CONCUSSIONS & CONSEQUENCES

THE PRESTON PLEVRETES STORY
and SECOND IMPACT SYNDROME

TAMMY BOURKE PLEVRETES

ISBN: 978-1-09837-928-5 (print)
ISBN: 978-1-09837-929-2 (eBook)

TABLE OF CONTENTS

ACKNOWLEDGEMENTS

"At times, our own light goes out and is rekindled by a spark from another person. Each of us has cause to think with deep gratitude of those who have lighted the flame within us."

—Albert Schweitzer

Throughout Preston's journey we have been blessed by the supreme dedication, unbound wisdom and caring support from so many people. To list all these wonderful people individually would constitute another book in itself. To all the doctors, nurses, aides, therapists, hospitals, organizations, family and friends, we appreciate and humbly thank you for providing your own nourishing "flame" that pulled us from the pits of grief and inspired hope to where we thought was none. I dedicate this book to all of you with sincere and abundant love.

CHAPTER 1

THE FOOTBALL FIELD

"Value the people who sacrifice something for you, because maybe that something was their everything."

—Unknown Author

The sun has made its early appearance over the treetops on this crisp fall morning, delivering its blinding but benevolent rays in my direction. A fresh blanket of morning fog hovers just above the damp, dewy grass of the football field, stimulating every one of my senses as I fully breathe in its earthly life. I find myself pleasantly aroused by the morning serenade provided by a chorus of unseen birds announcing the new day's vitality from somewhere among the branches of the nearby trees. I have been here to this place before, way too many times, sometimes positioning myself on the metal bleachers about eight rows up, center, closely parallel to the 50-yard line. I have never really paid much mind to the delightful artistry and elegance of this kind of early morning pastel, the leaves changing with the season, the whole scene looking so much like a watercolor painting; somehow even the turf looks greener than it does in summer. And yet, on this morning I realize with not a little surprise, that I never before noticed how rigid and cold these uncomfortable and unforgiving aluminum benches really are. Perhaps that's because, while certainly meant for sitting, I rarely sat upon them. My presence, and my attention was either somewhere down on that field making announcements, playing music in-between plays or working at the snack shack.

Yet on this halcyon, quiet morning, I really don't know why I am here. *Why would I bring myself to this bittersweet place,* I wondered? I close my eyes and attempt to find the rhythm of my breath and focus on nature's mantra to disconnect from the ever-so-present and unwanted chatter of my conscience that screams those words, "would of," "could of," and "should of"; those infernal words that play over and over again in my mind. Off in the distance I hear the sound of raucous laughter—just like Preston's—suddenly penetrating this moment of internal remorse, but I know it is not him. My attention is drawn to a group of young boys over by the goalpost, all dressed in their football uniforms, guffawing and preparing to start practice. Their unsuspecting parents are standing by the chain linked fence with coffee cups in hand, perhaps boasting to each other about their sons' courageous accomplishments achieved on that 120-yard battlefield, or perhaps second-guessing how grossly incompetent the coaches are—while never lifting a finger to volunteer as coaches themselves.

Yes, I have been here before, too many times before. Unfortunately, I know all too well that among that gathering of parents there are, as there will always be, any number of "helicopter" fathers—and less surprisingly these days, some helicopter mothers too. They are the ones who stand off to the side of the football field with their arms folded strategically across their chests as if in a display of defiance; the resentful ones who corner the coaches spewing arguments about why their boy should be the one playing a certain position or participating more in game play.

But on this pristine morning, I can only watch this scene with such heartbreak, deep bitterness, and humbling defeat. I want to run down from these bleachers and over to the coaches and the parents and talk some sense to them. I want to throw my hands on their shoulders and shake them to their very core so they will understand, to somehow get through to them. I want, selfishly perhaps, to make them to feel my anguish and my pain so they will reconsider what they are doing; what they are exposing their children to. I want to tell them how things are, how they *really* are and that I once walked in their shoes unknowing the very real and present dangers of this unforgiving game of football.

As I anxiously and painfully pose in utter contempt upon these empty unkind stands, vivid memories callously and maliciously flood my every thought as I observe the merciless practices down on that gridiron of battle. Some of those memories I graciously want to hold onto forever, while others I want to completely erase from my consciousness.

I struggle with this every single day of my life, but especially today, as I watch those young boys by the goalpost suiting up and preparing to face the fearless lesson of the battle without the forewarning of the potential consequences they may have to endure for the rest of their lives, whether physical, emotional, or both. Every hair on my body stands to attention as my hands grip tightly onto that relentlessly cold, harsh bench. My head fills with dreaded anticipation as I watch the all too familiar ritual of two boys ready to take the field as they grab onto each other's shoulder pads, facing each other as they vigorously jog in place, both yelling aggressively into each other's face that virile male sound of the animal "GROWLLLLL" like some kind of a primal scream. As this outwardly barbaric custom is acted out–presumably to stimulate the rush of adrenaline in these players—this ritual achieves its climax with the incomprehensibly violent—and downright dangerous—force filled blow known to footballers everywhere as the helmet-to-helmet head-butt!

I want to climb to the top of the goalposts that reach towards the heaven and scream at the top of my lungs and from the depths of my soul:

"STOP!!!! You don't know what you are doing!"

So tough and so proud and so indestructible, these young boys believe they are as I lament to myself in frustration, the abject futility of trying to get through to them—*both* the young players *and* their unmindful parents.

For I have memories of another boy, my boy, a gridiron gladiator who took to the fresh morning turf like a roaring tiger, just like those boys down there are doing now; with their childhood innocence and their fierce ambitions to be men of action and consequence, to be Brothers in Arms on the battlefield. Yet for that other young man I know, his consequence is that his life-long dreams have all but perished. As for his future… well. On this exquisite morning as the brilliant sunrise chases away the darkness, it takes all of the power of my inner spirituality to affirm that his future is optimistically undetermined, but nevertheless, filled with fearless, undaunted glorious hope.

PART I

Preston's Story

"I firmly believe that any man's finest hour, the greatest fulfillment of all that he holds dear, is that moment when he has worked his heart out in a good cause and lies exhausted on the field of battle - victorious."

—Vince Lombardi

Time, it travels in only a single direction, you can't change it, reverse it, or revisit it. Time can even play tricks on you with its droll wicked perception of speeding up or slowing down. And like a thief, time can even rob you of your precious memories evaporating them into a misty vapor then dissipating into thin air, gone forever. However, I cannot help but to wish that I had some sort of magical power to go back in time to the days before November 5, 2005 and fix all the mistakes that were made by so many, and that still relentlessly tear me apart these 14 years later. The portrait of my beautiful son arouses painful memories that time has yet to steal leaving me to view the heartbreaking loneliness of his empty days gradually fading into the past like the circadian mellow glow of the setting sun.

Preston is sitting in his wheelchair, silent and motionless, alongside the kitchen table. The bright sunshine that cascades through the sliding glass doors to the deck outside envelopes my oldest son in silhouette, obscuring the colors like an old sepia photograph. There is an eerie, almost ominous stillness about this scene that makes it simply heart-wrenching to look upon. Gazing at him, from my vantage point at the end of the long hallway, lingering there as I'm carrying a load of laundry to be washed, I wonder what he must be thinking about, as he sits there, all by himself amid the warming, yet somehow desperately cold sunshine. What is he feeling at this moment?

I imagine perhaps he is listening to the birds as they chirp madly, watching them as they flit about in frantic activity on the other side of the glass. Or else, as he sits in that almost celestial aura of light, perhaps he is reflecting, reliving in his mind the days when he would without a doubt be outside as well, on a lush field of thick green turf somewhere, tossing a football around with his friends, horsing around, doing their best to show off if any girls happened to be around. Or perhaps he is reliving something else altogether; the violent and brutal combat, and the sheer adrenaline-driven glory of Game Day.

But as Preston sits and stares blankly beyond those glass doors to the world outside, he seems so profoundly and unimaginably alone.

It is difficult, perhaps impossible, to know or understand what Preston is thinking or feeling these days. I close my eyes and think back to the happy and halcyon times before his horrific and devastating injury, and I can still see him with all his friends sitting around that same kitchen table joking, laughing, needling one another, and boisterously talking about football, cars, and girls, and what they want to do in life.

He should be with his friends, even now, experiencing and living the life of a carefree young man and figuring out how to live his life. Experiencing the passion of life's joys and sorrows, its successes and failures, and those triumphs over failures, too—and perhaps feeling the tender love of another, special person. Not sitting at home with his parents, almost lifeless, and staring, randomly it would seem, into the abyss of an uncertain, but limited future. Perhaps tragically, the loneliest of futures humanly imaginable.

These days, while Preston's face appears to bear the perpetual yet mystifying expression of a benign smile, there is yet an unnatural, disordered aspect in his countenance, one of pained grimace, of a damaged mind that longs to speak out and be heard but can't. Whether he is happy, or not, is as unknowable as any of his thoughts or dreams.

All of this is the massive, life-altering consequence of a tragic, catastrophic injury sustained in a collegiate football game. A catastrophic, nearly fatal brain injury that, in multiple, intuitively obvious, and unquestionably simple ways, could easily have been avoided.

CHAPTER 2

A PORTRAIT OF PRESTON
AS A YOUNG MAN

Weighing in at 9lb/3oz, 22 inches long at birth, my oldest son Preston Plevretes came into the world big, and he just kept on growing, consistently registering in the 90 to 95 percent rate on the standard growth chart. This singular though by no means unusual characteristic would have a subtle but significant impact on his life, particularly as it pertained to the earliest days of his involvement in organized sports; and most specifically, football.

What Preston's size meant in practical terms was that during his Pop Warner years beginning from the age of seven he was routinely deemed too big to play at the same level as other kids his age. Consequently, from his very first season, he entirely skipped the Mitey-Mite level of 7-9 year-olds and was placed in the Jr., Pee-Wee division, a multi-layer of 8, 9, and 10 year old boys. This level may also include 11-year-old boys who, while older, are lighter in weight or smaller in stature, and thus allowed to be on the team. Preston would continue to be bumped to the next higher level in a Pop Warner placement system governed as much by weight and size as it is by age. So, what does all this mean? While this adjustment might seem to make perfect sense on the surface, it is important to understand that in sports—and contact sports in particular—size alone does not determine one's readiness or suitability to advance to a given higher, more sophisticated—and a more physically demanding—level of play.

I had concerns about this as a mother, not simply because these boys were a year or two older than Preston, but because they had been playing the game for as much as two full years already, whereas Preston was just beginning. In other words, they had much more experience in how to play the game. In football of course, that means knowing how to most effectively hit, and tackle, and block opposing players, but it also means knowing how to take a hard hit when you the one being tackled and learning ways to try to minimize the impact—or to move in such a way as to avoid the impact entirely. Preston was going out there essentially blind, with no knowledge whatsoever of these important survival skills.

My fear was that he was going to get pounded because he was younger, and more directly as a consequence of being inexperienced. And that fear was warranted, because he was indeed pounded; and his physical dimensions simply did not make up for his lack of maturity as a player. In fact, there was one point when one of his coaches actually took the time to come to my husband Ted and me to suggest, out of genuine concern for Preston's safety and well-being, that maybe football might not the best sport for him.

A former semi-pro football player himself, Ted did not agree. Rather, he felt that Preston was just learning, and that it would take time for him to catch up with the others. But he also firmly believed that playing against the older, savvier boys would not only serve to make Preston better, and tougher, but would eventually make him one of the best players on the field by the time he reached high school. And in point of fact, even as he got pounded, which as a mother I found hard to watch, Preston excelled and developed a devoted passion in what quickly became his favorite sport. With each game he played, week after week, he honed and applied his rapidly developing skills, and he got better and better. Both his father and I had to admire how he became a true student of the game that he would eventually master. So too, and perhaps more than anyone else, did his younger brother Perry, who would grow up trying to emulate Preston in every way.

And by the time Preston was ready for high school, he was one of the best players on the field.

He became an immediate standout at Marlboro High School in New Jersey, where he played on the varsity squad right from his sophomore year and was awarded Offensive Player of the Year in football in his freshman, sophomore, junior, and senior years. But that, literally, only tells half of the story, because Preston was one of those rare, highly talented individuals capable of playing extraordinarily well on both sides of the ball. So, throughout his high school career, Preston regularly lined up on both offense and defense, which meant that he rarely came out of the game. Typically, his coaches would take him out to rest—for one play—and then he'd be right back on the field again. It wasn't unusual for Preston to play virtually all 48 minutes (the high-school standard) of a hotly contested game. Of course, any time that Preston was not in the game, he would be so pumped up that he would actually get in the face of his coaches to put him back in. He loved the adrenalin rush and the sheer excitement of the game. And while it was no surprise when he was elected a captain of the high school football team in his senior year, his athletic prowess was not limited to the gridiron.

Preston was also made a captain of the spring track team; he was such a natural in the javelin throw that he had hopes with proper training of representing the U.S. in the Olympics one day. At one track meet, a coach from one of the opposing schools actually came over and started working with Preston, giving him some helpful pointers on technique because, as he told Preston, "You've got talent." He also played basketball in his younger years, going so far as to participate in the International Basketball games in Puerto Rico, as well as playing on his high school team during his freshman and sophomore year. While not a bad player by any means, he understood that basketball was not his best sport, so he decided to concentrate and put everything he had into playing football. Even though the Marlboro Mustangs was not the best of teams, Preston himself was a standout and he earned a position to play not only in the local Divisional All-Star Game but also in the 2nd Annual University of South Florida's All-Star Classic Game in Tampa, sponsored by the Nationwide Athletic Recruiting Service, as a top recruit from New Jersey. This game featured some of the best athletes from across the United States as well as from a couple of European countries.

In Preston's room at home, displayed in a wobbly, old 3'-by-5' TV cabinet, are many football accolades and trophies, yet right alongside them are also many awards from other sports, including basketball, baseball, soccer as well as many distinguished medals in Javelin (his second favorite sport) and the shot put. Of course, how can I forget the belts he earned in Taekwondo during the Teenage Mutant Ninja Turtles era during his younger years. This display of awards is a disheartening reminder of a boy's life filled with vibrant hopes, dreams and aspirations. It became too hard to bear, it no longer exists.

Our younger son Perry followed his big brother's lead in playing multiple sports as well, which led to my two boys developing a close relationship based on their equal love and devotion for sports.

By the time he was 17 years old, Preston stood 6'2" and weighed 225 pounds, with piercing blue-green eyes, sandy-blonde hair, and not an ounce of extraneous fat anywhere in his entire body. His chiseled physique resembled that of the Greek God Arês (his birth sign), the God of War and one of the great Olympian Gods of the Greeks. Preston shares a Greek heritage with his father, and absolutely no one who observed his ferocious combat on the football field would have ever disputed the comparison to the God of War, especially Preston himself!

Yet Preston's impressive stature as a human being was not limited to his physical dimensions, or to his abundant and gifted athletic abilities. Simply put, Preston was one of those rare individuals who possess such an enormously gregarious personality and social charisma that it becomes infectious to everyone around them. One of those remarkably self-confident kids who, for example, whenever a rolling video camera would find his handsome, perfectly proportioned face—his smile instantly creating two irresistible dimples like opposing question marks—winks at the camera like a seasoned and unabashed veteran of the spotlight, as if betokening a sort of whimsical wisdom and a maturity far beyond his years.

Needless to say, it was the kind of thing that made all the girls melt. One evening after spending the day at the beach with his friends, mostly his football teammates, Preston was standing in the kitchen emptying his pockets. Along with the car keys and some loose change, a bunch of small, crumpled papers the size of post-it notes came spilling out onto the counter.

Curious, I asked him, "What are those?"

"Oh," Preston shrugged matter-of-factly, "Those are from some girls that gave me their phone numbers."

"But Preston" I said inquisitively, "You already have a girlfriend."

"So?" he replied in a matter-of-fact way as he jammed a loaded sub-sandwich into his mouth.

Dumbfounded by this response and as a loyal member of the female sect I stood there for a moment thinking God bless the girl who should ever fall for this boy. But if Preston ever needed any empirical proof of his popularity as admired football star (to both students and faculty), as a babe-magnet, and all around "big man on campus," he received daily validation of these facts simply by walking the halls of Marlboro High. I learned this firsthand one day when I had occasion to accompany my oldest son to his school late in his senior year.

Preston needed $200 cash only to purchase two tickets for him and his girlfriend to attend the senior prom. I was reluctant to simply hand the money over to him at home, because I knew what he would probably do with it. He'd very likely spend a healthy portion of that ready cash burning a hole in his pocket on something else—perhaps later on lamenting (or protesting covertly) that he had somehow, as a dutiful son, spent it on gasoline to fill the tank in one of our cars—and then he would ask me for more money to make up the underage for the prom tickets. (He was, after all, still a teenager at heart!) Knowing that trick all too well since I have fallen victim before, I decided to bring the money to the school, cut out the dubious middleman, and give it directly to the prom director myself, in person. I set up a time to meet Preston at school so that together we could officially complete the transaction.

We met at the appointed time, and together we walked down this long, quiet hall where classes were in session, the students presumably working hard at their lessons (or not!). But the classroom doors were all open, and with each one we passed, the teachers, one after another as if it were some sort of drill, stopped what they were doing, sometimes even in mid-sentence. And each one of them smiled broadly and waved through the open doorways and called out a hearty "Hey Preston" as we passed by! Incredible.

I could only stare at my son in wide-eyed, almost disbelieving amazement and puzzlement: these teachers were actually interrupting their teaching protocols to greet Preston!

And Preston, easily sensing my incredulity, smiled seductively, along with that cunningly mischievous twinkle in his eyes, hands out to the side, palms up and staring me directly in the face and said without blinking an eye, "I run this school."

I was completely dumbfounded; at first, I could not tell if he was joking or not. He stood there like a pretentious teenager waiting for some kind of reaction from me. But then he started laughing, almost nervously, perhaps sensing my consternation, and gently bumping his sinewy shoulder into me, he reassured, "Oh come on mom, I'm just kidding!" and he laughed some more as he continued on his way, his laughter echoing loudly down the hallway. Then he turned and gave me a jaunty wink, which rendered me immobile for a moment and left me questioning if, in fact, he really was kidding!

Still, you had to admire that kind of monumental, monstrous self-assurance in a young man soon to embark on his own journey, to college and beyond. One thing was abundantly clear: Preston was a respected and admired leader and he relished in this position. Moreover, it was further obvious that even the Marlboro High School administrators recognized these qualities in Preston when they approached him to become a member of the school's Peer Leadership program. And fortunately, for all of his playfulness—and devilishness—he nevertheless remained personally humble and respectful of others. At least I hoped this was so. He was, by anyone's account, pretty much a good kid all around.

Finally, as if all of that wasn't enough, Preston had, on his own, and without any prodding from his parents, devised a very responsible and practical proactive plan for his life that was as deliberate and definitive as it was ambitious. In part due to his desire to stay relatively close to home, Preston chose to attend La Salle University in the bustling city of Philadelphia, where of course he would play college football over his four years while he earned his BA. His plan from there was to play football at the supreme level in the National Football League—if he could make the grade—or play for a period of four or five years in the European leagues, or perhaps play professional Arena football in the U.S. if he fell short of his NFL aspirations. That's how much he loved the game. Whatever his fortunes in the sport of football might have turned out to be, Preston also planned, absolutely, to participate in the Olympics in the javelin competition.

Yet even at that young age, Preston was circumspect and wise enough to understand that there would be a lot of life left for him after football as a career, and that he was obliged to have a plan for that phase as well. He did, and that part of his plan was to settle in with a "real" job as a broadcast sports announcer with ESPN. At La Salle he chose to major in Communications and Broadcasting with this specific and decisive goal in mind.

It bears underscoring just how firmly and soberly grounded in objective reality Preston's plans and expectations for his life truly were. Well aware of the of the rarified skill set, and—let's face it—the sheer, outright, withering good luck it takes to become one of the elite players that make it into the NFL, his consciously calculated back-up plans for playing in Europe or an Arena league here at home were both solidly within his reach. In the longer term, with his gregarious personality, an easy-going, friendly nature that put other people at ease, and his expansive sense of humor, Preston fully realized that the TV sports broadcast booth covering the sport he loved as analyst or play-by-play commentator would be the ideal life-long career for him. He would have been a natural there, just as he was on the field as a player. I firmly believe without a doubt that he would have accomplished his dreams.

Ted and I both felt these objectives sounded really good, very solidly thought out, and perfectly reasonably attainable plan. And any parent will tell you what a gratifying joy it is when your children seem to know precisely what it is they want to do with their lives, when they seem to have it all together—not for the sake of your own happiness, but wholly for the sake of theirs.

Truth was, in this day and age and economic reality, I was thrilled that he would be able to support himself and find his own way, and not be forced by circumstance to live at home after college for a span of time before being able to get fully out on his own two feet. Of course, for his part, Ted was downright euphoric over Preston's plan, since he worships the game of football and always took his greatest delight in watching both of our boy's play.

And so, in late August of 2004, the big charismatic kid and football star from Marlboro High, the budding, fine young man with big aspirations and the world on a string, at last left home to go off to college at LaSalle University.

* * * * *

Box 2.1. Clash of the Plevretes

Whether it might be blamed on the Greek heritage in his blood or on the favorable treatment and adulation heaped upon him by his coaches and trainers (which was much more likely the source), Preston sometimes acted very much as though he was indeed some kind of powerful and willful God—and often very much to my utter dismay and firm disapproval. And while teenagers and their parents often collide over behavioral issues, Preston's deistic attitude gave added dimension to the "Clash of the Plevretes." Whenever that happened, I would call him out on it, demanding that he leave that detestable, self-exalting attitude on the field where it belonged and not bring it into our home.

"There is no place in this house for rudeness and arrogance," I told him many times, "and you are not a god around here!" I added, just as a reminder.

"Oh mom," he would say, deliberately using that impish smile punctuated by those sweet dimples, and his handsome looks, to devastating and deeply sinister effect, as he melted back down into feigned boyish innocence.

And like any other teenager, Preston quickly became adept at pushing my buttons; like when he would follow me everywhere around the house with the camcorder placed roughly two inches from my face videotaping me while I was trying to do everyday chores like washing the dishes or doing the laundry. Most incorrigible of all, when he realized I was angry with him for some reason, suddenly his eyes would zone in on me, the hint of a diabolical smile curling his lips, as he positioned himself in the football set position—the dreaded three-point stance—kicking up one heel, then the other, each time snorting like a bull ready to charge. Then I knew, I knew what was coming.

"Don't you dare do it!" I'd command in the sternest voice I could muster, trying desperately to suppress the laughter that was bubbling up in my chest. "I'm telling you, I wouldn't do it if I were you" again hurling my firm parental voice. But it was no use.

"Hut one. Hut two…. HUT!" and with that he would charge toward me like a blitzing linebacker, throwing me bent at the torso over one of his massive shoulders and dizzily spinning around the living room like a top, then bounding up the stairs and back down again, the whole time I'm screaming at him to "put me down you fool!"—when I can manage to blurt the words out through my breathless laughing—until he finally plunges me down onto the couch like an old disheveled rag doll.

And of course by this time, as he had impishly planned, erased completely and irretrievably from my memory anything about what the hell I was angry about in the first place. I invariably ended up just plain exhausted from the sheer delightful panic of the footballer's dance and so woozy with laughter that I'm struggling just to breathe enough oxygen to remain among the living. He knew just how to make me laugh, and he also knew that there was absolutely nothing I could do to stop him from making me laugh. But Preston was also very caring, lovable, and extremely funny. While I could never really be mad at him for very long (and I tried, believe me I tried), those are some the characteristics of his personality that I truly miss today.

Senior Picture

Marlbor H.S. Senior Linebacker

I've just been tackled

At the Beach

Preston & Perry

CHAPTER 3

THE FIRST HIT

If I have painted too rosy a picture of my "ideal" first son, let me clarify that he was in many ways just as aggravatingly incorrigible as any other kids his age, with some of the same faults that so many teenage boys are prone. Particularly the ones who think themselves invincible, which I've come to believe is almost all of them, at one point or another. Suffice it to say, it wasn't easy living with a self-imposed "god." I remember one time, after complaining at length to my own mother about my son's sometimes belligerent and disobedient behavior, that I prophesized quite unknowingly to his Grandmother that one day Preston would get his comeuppance. It's a remark that I deeply regret, and I will forever have to live with the gnawing guilt of ever having uttered it.

Regrettably, Preston was not by any means the best of students, academically. In being fully devoted to fulfilling his essential roles of Marlboro High's leading sports hero, "social butterfly," and all-around big-man-on-campus, Preston's grades suffered, and his lackluster academic performance had an adverse impact on his choice of colleges, in particular, by limiting his opportunities among NCAA Division I schools. Those universities with the marquee intercollegiate sports programs generally required incoming freshmen to have achieved a 2.0 or C average in high school in order to be eligible to play. Not to say that several of them did not actively seek out Preston as a candidate; they certainly did. However, with his low-grade average he could be a risk as to whether he would be eligible to play, and as a consequence, they moved on to more academically stable athletes. It must be noted that the NCAA in 2015 did change the requirements to a 2.3 GPA in 16 core courses (up from 2.0 in 13 courses). In addition, this controversial change states that ten of those courses must be completed within the first three years of high school in order to be eligible to compete as a freshman and no courses can be retaken for a better grade.

Preston, however, finished high school with a disappointing 1.9 GPA, a letter C average, and that played into his decision, finally, to attend LaSalle, along with his desire to stay close—but not too close—to home.

Even at LaSalle's NCAA Division 2 Football program, Preston's low-grade point average meant that he missed the eligibility cut of 2.0 GPA that was required at the time by a single percentage point, so he had to redshirt his first year so that he could work on raising his grades to meet the academic standard required to be permitted to play on the university's football team. Redshirting meant that Preston could practice with the team and be with his teammates on the sidelines during games, but he was not permitted to play, and it also meant that he would retain his full four years of eligibility over his college career. In fact, unbeknownst to either Ted or me, Preston quietly hired a couple of tutors to help him in that effort. Of course, if as concerned parents we might have been gratified and proud of our son for exhibiting the maturity and good sense to do that for himself and all on his own, those emotions had to be tempered by the ever-present knowledge that he was, in reality, doing all of these wonderful things only in service to the ultimate goal in his life— which of course was playing football on the next level.

It wasn't until years later, and long after his catastrophic brain injury, that I would finally learn how Preston was able to pay for his tutors. One very typical morning, as he and I were sitting at the kitchen table enjoying our breakfast along with his daytime aide Lena, and just before leaving for his daily rehabilitation appointment, Preston revealed quite openly to both of us the slightly humorous, yet the "shocking truth"—as the media tabloids like to say—surrounding his secret fundraising campaign.

I am not sure how we got onto this subject, but we were talking about the unfortunate reality that Preston would probably never marry and never experience the joys and gratification of becoming a father. With this, however, Preston only smiled coyly and then leaned deliberately forward in his wheelchair to a point where the sun's rays penetrating through the glass doors sparked that distinctive, mischievous twinkle in his eyes. Having thus gotten our attention, he slyly began to reveal his dirty little money-making scheme with a provocatively wicked question.

"How do you know that I am not already a father?" he asked probingly, looking for all the world like the proverbial evil villain with a dark and diabolical secret.

The room became quiet and still; the atmosphere dense with numbness, as Preston's strange and unnerving question hung in the air. After startling us with—what was this? Some sort of astonishing and as-yet unrevealed news? —he relaxed back in his wheelchair with self-satisfaction in his face, obviously delighted with my stunned and speechless reaction—at least initially. Lena and I could only look at each other, completely dumbfounded. Even as I anticipated a reasonable explanation for this outrageous question, I experienced a very uneasy feeling inside, physically and emotionally, as I pondered the question, *do I really want to discover that I might actually have a grandchild somewhere out there?*

I summoned my courage, and through narrowing eyes I said, "Really Preston! Now just what do you mean by that comment?"

With obvious amusement and satisfaction that had just thrown me for a loop, just the way he had always enjoyed doing to me since he was a little boy, Preston replied with only two little words.

"Sperm bank!" he said, then sat back in his chair and curiously waited for my bemused reaction.

After a shuddering moment of silence while I struggled to process what he had so unabashedly just declared, and utterly aghast as the full realization came into focus, I replied, "Ahhh, excuse me? What!?"

He smiled broadly, sporting his charming boyish dimples, and then he went on to explain—the fact that Preston's speech can be very difficult to distinguish only made his protracted explanation all the more wildly hysterical, at least in the moment. Briefly stated, while he was attending LaSalle, Preston had hit upon the "brilliant" idea that he could earn some money by making deposits at the local sperm bank. And while he refused to reveal how many times he went there (or maybe he didn't remember!), he explained that he was paid $50 for each, shall we say, installment. Of course, it goes without saying I guess, that a healthy 19- or 20-year-old male could conceivably make quite a bit of money by doing this.

While I was downright appalled at this startling revelation, I found that I could not really be cross or upset with Preston concerning any of the obvious implications of what he had done. Especially not after everything he had been through in his young life. More soberly, however, I could not help but to think, that if this surprising information was indeed true—and I had no reason to doubt him—it would only further serve to prove that there was absolutely nothing Preston wouldn't do to get himself back on that football field.

Although it must also be said that in finally digging into his studies, Preston developed a surprising love for history, which became one of his favorite classes, and overall, he did start to take his studies more seriously. And thankfully, his grades did improve substantially over the course of the year. Out on the football field, however, Preston watched as the LaSalle Explorers compiled a 3-7 won-loss record, all the while gritting his teeth for the opportunity that would come the following season when, as an eligible sophomore, he hoped he would be able to play a major role in turning the team's fortunes around.

However, Preston's much anticipated inaugural season as a starting defensive linebacker got off to something of an inauspicious start that, in hindsight, would reveal a shocking glimpse into how different types of athletic injuries are prioritized. The first week of August, in a practice session even before playing in his first college game, Preston sustained an injury to his right hand when it was hit hard by another player's helmet. Almost immediately, the hand became swollen and sore, and painful to touch when LaSufe an employee of La Salle's athletic department manipulated it in his efforts to diagnose the injury, at least preliminarily, and fearing that Preston may have broken one of the metacarpal bones in the hand. Initially, X-rays taken at

Philadelphia's Germantown Hospital proved negative, a fact that may have been due to the swelling of the tissue; and the doctors there indicated that Preston had a severely sprained hand. He was cleared to play, and to continue to practice, although LaSufe instructed that he should wear a protective hard-foam pad bandaged over the afflicted hand.

When the pain continued, however, somewhere around September 8th LaSufe sent Preston to the Einstein Orthopedics medical group. A new set of X-rays taken of the hand revealed what was described as a "boxer's fracture" of the fifth metacarpal, which the attending physician, orthopedist and hand specialist Dr. Hirsh, treated by "reducing the fracture," presumably by manipulating the broken bone back into place, and by putting the hand into a hard cast. Nonetheless, Dr. Hirsh cleared Preston to play even with the cast, while also scheduling him for surgery to insert a temporary steel pin to correct the alignment the 5th finger, which Preston was having trouble extending due to the fracture. That surgery was performed on the 14th of September, where-after the hand was re-casted, and once again, the doctor cleared Preston to play, with a fracture, steel pin, hard cast and all. Finally, Dr. Hirsh performed one more surgery to remove the pin on October 18th, instructing that while Preston could do some running exercises the following day, he should not engage in any live-action team activities or physical contact drills for 24 hours. LaSufe accompanied Preston on many, if not all, of his visits with Dr. Hirsh, and after that very short interval, Preston was once again cleared—by the physician—for full team practice activities and play in actual games.

The illuminating relevance of this brief history of Preston's relatively minor hand injury—indeed, something that might be regarded as a nuisance "flesh wound" to the tough-as-nails, incredibly resilient, and defiantly injury-ignoring young men that play this sport—will become clear in the following pages. But the fact is that a broken metacarpal that received so much "hands on" attention (no pun intended) from the La Salle athletic department was not the most severe injury that Preston would suffer before his collegiate career had barely gotten started. Not by a longshot.

* * * * *

In a practice session on Tuesday, October 4th, Preston was head butted helmet to helmet by another player at a distance of about 5 yards. Preston likely thought little of it at the time; after all, throughout his Pop Warner and high school playing days he had been knocked around quite a bit, and to his mind that just came with the territory. However, the following Saturday, October 8th, playing in an away game in Poughkeepsie against Marist College—a lopsided 27-0 loss—Preston pulled himself out of the game in the middle of the fourth quarter. He told LaSufe that he just "didn't feel right." More specifically, Preston reported that every time he hit, or was hit by another player, whether in making a tackle or fending off an opposing block, he felt a quick, severe pain shoot through his head. "I'm getting headaches," he tried to explain. For Preston to pull himself out of a game, he must have been very concerned that something was wrong. And that's when he told LaSufe about the helmet-to-helmet hit that had occurred in practice four days earlier. On the sideline, LaSufe asked Preston a few orientation questions, briefly checked out his eyes, and suspecting a possible concussion, took Preston out for the remaining, dwindling minutes of a game that was already a lost cause. He performed no other sideline tests, such as having Preston do exertion exercises, to try to determine the potential extent or seriousness of his injury.

For reasons that are unclear to this day, LaSufe also apparently decided that Preston's complaints were not serious enough to have him looked at by a doctor. In fact, this may have been in part because, being an away game, that would have involved the extra step of taking my son over to the opposite sideline to see the covering physician from Marist College. That's because among the smaller (and less wealthy) collegiate football programs, like those of virtually all of the schools in the Metro Atlantic Athletic Conference (MAAC) of which La Salle was a member, it was customary for the home team to have their own doctor or team physician present and available on game days, thus saving the visiting team the added expense of traveling their doctor to the game. Instead, LaSufe told Preston to go lie down in the team bus.

When the game was over, Preston rode back to the La Salle campus on the team bus along with all of his teammates; LaSufe traveled back to the school separately, in a van along with other members of the coaching staff.

On the following day of October 9th, when Preston met briefly with LaSufe, he asked him if he still had a headache.

"A mild one," Preston reported.

Whereupon, LaSufe would later claim in court papers, he handed Preston a boilerplate concussion warning sheet; which is to say, a sheet of paper that listed all of the usual warning signs of a potential concussion injury, and further claimed that he instructed Preston to "put this up on your refrigerator," and to let his roommates know that the warning sheet was posted on the refrigerator door. Aside from informing Preston himself, presumably this was to alert Preston's roommates should they happen to notice Preston displaying any of the symptoms listed on the sheet. I personally do not recall noticing any paper of this sort on the refrigerator at Preston's place, or as an inquisitive mother I would have questioned it on one of our visits. Therefore, I have always doubted that LaSufe ever actually gave Preston the warning sheet, given his overall negligence in regard to Preston's medical care.

However, LaSufe would later admit in court testimony that nowhere in his player-injury case notes that there was any specific indication that this warning sheet was actually given to Preston. He then instructed Preston to go to the University's Student Health Center when they opened on Monday. However, at that brief post-game meeting, LaSufe did not ask Preston a single question about the original head-butting incident on the practice field back on October 4th, and once again he performed no further tests to try to determine the nature and extent of Preston's injury.

So on Monday morning as ordered, Preston duly arrived at the Student Health Center where he was seen by Ms. Shcemp, and told her about the continuing intermittent headaches he had been experiencing since the head-butting incident. In her efforts to evaluate Preston's condition, Shcemp closely examined Preston's head and neck to check for any physical signs of injury, from contusions to possible fracture of the skull to strain of the neck muscles. Shcemp also tested Preston's hearing and eyesight, as well as his heart rate and balance, and found no abnormalities. In fact, all of her tests proved negative for any serious injury. However, she also administered what she would later describe as her own version of what is known as the

Standardized Assessment of Concussion, or SAC test. This was outrageous! Since La Salle's Student Health Center did not purchase the SAC kit, Shcemp took it upon herself and created her own adaptive version from some spurious place off the internet.

Adding further insult, she was using the Cantu grading scale from 1986! (The Cantu Grading Scale is a system for gauging the severity of concussions developed by Dr. Robert Cantu, perhaps the leading concussion injury experts in the nation. Dr. Cantu's evaluation of Preston's case follows later in this book.) You would think that with football being such a ferocious game these institutions would require more detailed testing and precautions to be completed before clearance to play to ensure that an athlete's health and life are protected. Briefly, the SAC test according to its creators is designed "to provide clinicians with a more objective and standardized method of immediately assessing an injured athlete's mental status *on the sports sideline within minutes* of having sustained a concussion." (emphasis mine) (http://ds.iris.edu/files/sac-manual)

However, as will be described in detail later in this book, Shcemp both conducted and scored the test incorrectly, although ultimately diagnosing Preston with a mild Grade 1 concussion. She did not refer him to be seen by a physician, and she did little else but to prescribe that Preston take Tylenol to try to relieve his headaches. What I find frustrating is that a concussion does not only include symptoms of chronic headache—which appears to be the only thing the student health people were concerned about with Preston, but also includes things like memory loss and cognitive impairment. Even further, a concussion can cause memory impairment to the point that patients may not even remember any of the other symptoms they are experiencing, or even how long they have suffered with these symptoms. In this way, the memory loss or impairment serves to "mask" any recognition of the other, equally serious symptoms.

Still, Shcemp concluded, largely if not solely based on the fact that Preston was still experiencing those headaches, that he remained symptomatic, and prescribed a plan wherein Preston was not to practice or play for one full week after his remaining symptoms of intermittent headaches had fully subsided. While it remained to be seen precisely when Preston's symptoms would be judged to have ceased, the one thing that was certain at this point in my football-loving son's mind was that he would be ineligible to play in the following Saturday's game.

* * * * *

La Salle University's campus in North Philadelphia was only about a two-hour drive from our home in Marlboro, and as Ted and I had always been devoted to supporting both of our boys in their athletic pursuits, we made the trip to Philadelphia to attend Preston's home games whenever we could. So, I was fairly surprised when Preston called that same Monday evening to tell me not to bother to come to the next Saturday's game because he would not be playing that day. Naturally, as any mother would be, I was deeply concerned when he told me that the reason was due to his having sustained a concussion, no matter how "mild" an event that might have been. However, my concern quickly turned to alarm, even outrage, when Preston informed me that neither the athletic department nor the Student Health Center staff had taken him to the hospital for appropriate testing or seen to it that he was examined by a doctor.

I was incredulous! I immediately told Preston to come home and we would take him directly to a doctor or an ER ourselves, but one way or another we were going to get him checked out.

Today when I think back on the profound failures of medical oversight both by the athletic department and the student health department, I recall the days when Preston was being recruited by LaSalle. In particular, I remember our meeting in 2003 with the head coach at the time, the late Archie Stalcup. Stalcup was a well-seasoned, very successful football coach who was also highly respected for his fairness on the field and his compassion for his players. I remember that when we met in Archie's windowless, dimly lit office, I purposefully sat tall, firmly positioned on the edge of my chair, because I wanted to make sure I listened attentively about the logistics of the team. Because I had questions to which I wanted specific, definitive answers. In particular, I questioned him about his protocol if there were to be an injury.

Coach Stalcup smiled warmly, and leaning forward, he reached over and turned a rather simple wooden framed picture that was sitting on his desk towards me. It was a picture of him standing with two young men dressed in their football uniforms. He then went on to say that these boys, his own sons, played football, and that he truly understood the fears and concerns of parents regarding the potential of injuries to their player-sons. Archie then assured me that he would take care of Preston "as if he were one of my own boys" he said.

I found his sincerity and compassion so reassuring that I even remember I was able to relax peacefully, sliding back comfortably into my chair. Regrettably, even as Coach Stalcup made that promise, he was facing medical issues of his own—issues that forced him to resign from LaSalle at the end of the year—and a new much younger coach was already in place when Preston was finally eligible to play in his sophomore year.

So, my son came home directly, and the very next day, on the eleventh, Ted and I took him first to the eye doctor for an eye exam and new contact lenses, and then Ted took him to the emergency room at CentreState Medical Center in Freehold, New Jersey, where he was examined by Dr. William Ross, D.O. The first thing Dr. Ross did was have Preston undergo a very basic, non-contrast CAT scan. While the injury or abnormality detection capabilities of a non-contrast CAT scan are markedly limited, in that it is primarily used to detect such serious conditions as brain swelling, bruising, or bleeding, any given brain scan is really also only a snapshot in time, and it may not detect changes, micro-bleeds or any other symptoms that might develop or evolve over time. Moreover, while Preston's CAT scan result was normal, it was not reviewed by a qualified neuro-radiologist who may have provided a different diagnosis, or who may have ordered further testing. Failing that, Dr. Ross' otherwise routine physical examination of Preston revealed no symptoms other than the same intermittent headaches Preston had reported to La Salle's Student Health Center.

While he was not willing to rule out the possibility, the likelihood in fact, that Preston had indeed suffered a concussion of some significant magnitude, the factual, medical results of his examination necessarily led him to conclude just short of that; that Preston was suffering with a post-traumatic headache or PTH. The International Headache Society defines PTH as "a headache developing within seven days of trauma or injury or after regaining consciousness" (though in Preston's case he never lost consciousness). It is worth noting that PTH is not just a plain and simple headache, but rather, it represents a more substantial side-effect resulting from a traumatic brain injury (TBI), whether mild or severe. Accordingly, in discharging Preston from the CentreState ER, Dr. Ross, or rather, one of his nurses, handed Ted a printed set of post-exam instructions for Preston that included, most importantly, the specific direction that Preston follow up within 2-3 days with an examination by either his own primary care doctor or another physician, presumably of course, La Salle University's attending physician.

It was the only extant copy of Doctor Ross' instructions, because at the time and again somewhat inexplicably, CentreState did not keep a record of patient follow-up instructions for its own internal files. But it gets even worse, because most disturbingly of all, CentreState had lost track of their own historical records, and thus failed to make available to Dr. Ross medical records that would have shown that Preston had been previously seen and diagnosed at CentreState with concussions in both 2000 and 2003! CentreState blamed this "glitch" on a recent switch-over to a new computer system at the facility, but clearly in Preston's case, knowledge of those previous incidents would have played a major role in Preston's diagnosis, significantly indicating the need for further testing. Records again went unnoticed, and my boy slipped through the cracks.

This is another regret that plagues me to this day; the fact that I did not go with Ted and Preston to the ER due to another obligation to which I was already committed. I am quite certain that I would have given more pertinent information about Preston's previous concussions because I was the one who accompanied him on those previous visits to CentreState to address those injuries.

After he returned to school the following day, Preston subsequently gave Dr. Ross' instructions for his immediate follow up care directly to LaSufe.

The instruction sheet would never be seen again.

One individual who would never even see Dr. Ross' follow-up instructions at all was Shcemp at the La Salle Student Health. In fact, she would later testify in a deposition that LaSufe had told her that the follow-up instructions that Preston had given him were actually a "clearance to play" from "Preston's doctor." LaSufe later admitted in court documents that he thought the paper that Preston had given him when he came back to school on the 12th was "a prescription pad note [from Dr. Ross] that Preston was cleared to play football." Strangely enough, LaSufe claimed that he could not find the paper bearing Dr. Ross' instructions. Still, LaSufe told Preston—regardless of what the papers Dr. Ross had given him said—that he still had to report back to Student Health before he could be cleared to play again. Once again, he failed to make sure that Preston was seen by a qualified doctor.

Another vexing question is this: Why didn't anybody bother to look in Preston's file and see the Concussion Information Form that was required by LaSalle to be completed before the season, which would have informed the Athletic Department about Preston's previous concussions? Athletes with a history of concussions are at a greater risk for future concussions and repeated concussions may cause more extensive brain damage. These are all factors that *must* be taken into serious consideration with regard to any decision to continue to let an athlete play—or to be prohibited from playing—whether for a single game or an entire season. Once again, Preston was allowed to slip through the cracks. Why did no one care for my son?

So, on Wednesday, October 12th and the day after his CAT scan, Preston reported back to Student Health where he was re-examined. Shcemp repeated her flawed administration of the SAC text, this time crediting Preston with a 100 percent score of 30 out of 30—a perfect score that the SAC test creators indicate in their literature is achieved by no more than seven percent of *normal* (i.e., non-brain injured) subjects. She asked Preston if he was still having headaches. Preston told her, quite hopefully in his own mind, that he had experienced his last headache on the previous morning—a few hours before his visit to CentreState Medical. But he also told her that he had been able to relieve that headache by taking Tylenol as prescribed.

And yet, it was on that basis, with Preston reporting no headache and no other symptoms at the moment as he sat in the Student Health Center office on the twelfth, that Shcemp declared that my son was asymptomatic and the clock could begin on his required period of no-practice no-play for one full week of seven days, per the athletic department's standard policy. Think about that: the Student Health Center employee gave no consideration whatsoever to the very strong possibility that it was only through the use of Tylenol—and we don't know how many pills Preston was taking—that my son had been able to manage his ongoing headaches through the previous day.

While he was not allowed to practice with the team during this observational term, LaSufe instructed Preston to begin performing exertional exercises, progressively increasing in intensity over the seven days and designed to test whether any of his symptoms might return. Or as LaSufe put it, the exertion exercises were progressively ramped up in part as a deliberative attempt to "elicit" the recurrence of symptoms; failure of that to occur, ostensibly, meant that Preston would have fully recovered from his injury. This is standard procedure in athletic circles, or it was at the time, but the important thing to note is that such increasing exertional exercise must be diligently followed and carefully monitored by an employee of the athletic department. One thing there is no doubt about; nobody could have been happier or more eager to get back out on the practice field than my football-loving son.

La Salle Football

* * * * *

As detailed later on in sworn testimony by LaSufe himself, Preston's exertion exercise progression went something like this:

On Thursday, October 13, LaSufe directed Preston to run, at a jog's pace and without wearing a helmet, around the football field for 20 minutes nonstop. When Preston had completed this task, LaSufe asked him how he was feeling; did he have a headache, or any dizziness or balance issues, or did he feel nauseous or the like. Preston said no.

Preston did the same thing on Friday—20 minutes of light jogging—this time and from hereafter through the progression period, wearing his helmet during his exertional exercises, again under the direction of the LaSufe, and again Preston expressed experiencing no noticeable return of his symptoms, according to the athletic department employee.

On Saturday, October 15, LaSufe was obliged to travel with the team to an away game against Catholic University in Washington, D.C. It was one of the Explorers' better showings, but nevertheless resulted in a 41-34 loss. As a consequence however, LaSufe did not see Preston at all that day, and whether, speculatively, my son might have done some light running or other athletic activity on his own, he did not perform any exertion exercises directly under the observation of the LaSufe.

Sunday, the 16th, being the day after a game, was typically an "off" day from practice for the team. For a second consecutive day, Preston performed no specific exertion exercises under the direct observation of LaSufe.

On Monday the 17th, and for the first time fully five days into his "seven-day progression" of the exertion exercise program, the intensity of Preston's exercise for the day was increased, albeit modestly, to "agility work," described by LaSufe as performing exercises such as linebacker-specific "back peddling and sports specific techniques with the team." It was also the first time that he was allowed to engage in non-contact practice alongside his teammates.

On Tuesday October 18, Preston had been scheduled to see Dr. Hirsh at Einstein Orthopedic to have the steel pin removed from his right hand. For the third day of his seven-day exertional progression, Preston engaged in no specific exercises under the direct observation of LaSufe or any employee of the athletic department.

On Wednesday October 19, under orders from Dr. Hirsh to allow a day for the minor surgery his hand to start to heal properly, Preston once again did not practice at all, and he engaged in no progressive exertional exercises under the direct observation of any employee of the athletic department, other than to do some light running around the practice field for an unspecified period of time.

And as incredible as it may seem, on Thursday, October 20 and as if by default, Preston was fully and officially cleared to play football once again. In fact, for reasons that have never been fully explained, LaSufe's own case history records indicate that he had officially cleared Preston to play in actual games on the 16th, only four days after Preston had been seen at Student Health Center and three days before his seven-day exertional exercise progression was completed. In court papers, LaSufe would claim that Preston had been cleared to play by Student Health, even though he never sent Preston back to Student Health again after the progression was complete. For their part, Shcemp testified that neither she nor anyone else at Student Health ever officially cleared Preston to play again—certainly not prematurely on the 16th, but she also conceded that neither did Student Health clear him on the 21st.

Throughout the entirety of his seven-day progression, Preston had not been directed by any athletic department employee to do any blood-pumping exercises that would effectively raise his heart rate and blood pressure. He was not tested by asking him to do a set of vigorous push-ups. No jumping jacks. No squats. No sit-ups. No deep knee bends. No calisthenics of any kind that might serve to apply pressure to his brain which in turn might reveal any continuing problems or the persistence of an injury. He was never sent to see LaSalle's doctor, nor had he ever been examined by any other competent doctor, nor of course, had he in any way, shape or form been medically cleared by one.

Unlike as he had done concerning Preston's hand injury, LaSufe never once accompanied my son to a doctor's office, nor even to the Student Health Center. I will think about it in anguish for the rest of my life; how utterly different things could have been for my charismatic oldest son if LaSufe had cared as much about preserving the critical health and safety of Preston's brain as he did about restoring the purely functional utility of his right hand specifically so that he could continue to play—even with the hand encased in a hard cast before it had fully healed.

* * * * *

The tragic truth in all of this, however, is that Preston's symptoms persisted throughout this entire time from the moment of the head-butting hit in early October. Hamm, who was one of his roommates, would later tell an ESPN television news team that Preston "was never symptom free."

"Not at all," Hamm continued, adding, "He was always complaining about having headaches." Hamm said that Preston was never right after the October 4th head-butting injury.

When the ESPN reporter asked the roommate how Preston dealt with the headaches, Hamm grimly replied, "Advil. Handfuls at a time."

Hamm's revelations about Preston's constant headaches were further confirmed by Candy, the young woman who Preston was dating during this time. Candy further acknowledged that not only did Preston complain often about having persistent headaches, but also that they were apparently very painful, throbbing headaches, noting that on several evenings when the two of them planned to go out together on a date, all Preston wanted to do with lie in his bed, quiet and motionless, trying desperately to manage the excruciating pain in his head.

In fact, several years later as I was going through Preston's records from his college days, I came across a chilling text message that Candy had sent to him on October 11, 2005—the same day that Ted took Preston to CentreState to be checked out. After describing some bizarre—and downright goofy—things that Preston had apparently said to her, Candy wrote, "Good thing you're getting a CAT scan today."

Why? Why didn't Preston's girlfriend, or anyone else for that matter, say anything to either Ted, or me, or anyone in the athletic department—or to *anyone?*

Such was the case when Ted and I visited the campus to attend the game on the twenty-ninth, after which we planned to take Preston and his roommates, and his girlfriend Candy, out to a nice dinner that evening. On that particular Saturday afternoon we were treated to a rare La Salle victory, and a nail-biting finish to boot, as La Salle's freshman kicker split the uprights with a 31-yard field goal with no time left on the game clock. The kick lifted Preston's team to a stunning 38-36 win over Kean University, and gave us all something terrific to celebrate at dinner that night.

However, toward the evening when we arrived at the boy's off-campus residence to collect everyone and head out to the restaurant, one of them informed us that Preston was upstairs in bed, in his room, with his girlfriend. Truth be told, I was a bit angry at my do-as-he–pleases son-god at this point. He was a grown man or thereabouts, away from home for the first time in his life and certainly free to make his own decisions, or so I supposed, but I couldn't help wondering what the heck he was doing up there with her, especially knowing that Ted and I would be shortly at his doorstep. I found it more than a little insulting. I had no idea, of course, that he was doing nothing other than lying in bed trying desperately to make the pain go away.

And to this day I wonder if I should have known; if I should have been able to put two and two together. Because that morning just as we were leaving for Philadelphia, I was talking with Preston on the phone and he asked me to bring him some Advil. When I asked what for, he explained that he and his friends were partying the night before, he'd had a little too much to drink— beer was his beverage of choice—and had awakened with a bad hangover. When we arrived and I handed him the bottle of Advil, I questioned him a bit more closely.

"You're not still getting headaches from the concussion, are you?" I asked pointedly. "No Mom!" he insisted, almost in strident protest of the motherly question, and maintaining the line that he simply had a hangover from partying the night before. And the truth was that for all Ted or I could tell from that point when we first saw him, and even when he and his girlfriend came gliding downstairs all smiles and we all went out to dinner, Preston seemed otherwise totally fine to us. I would not learn until much later on, from his girlfriend's sworn testimony in the litigation that was to come, that Preston had an unwavering rule that he would not drink alcohol for at least three to four days before a game. How I wish that she, or one of his roommates, had told us how Preston was continually suffering with those headaches.

It's unfortunate and unfair, and sometimes tragically so, but one of the pitfalls that all parents face comes when you send your children away to school and they are no longer living under your roof and knowing that you will not be able to see what they are up to, and who their friends are, and what struggles they may be experiencing. And the most frustrating thing of all, is when you try to ask them how things are going, they lie!

In any event, somehow Preston managed to practice full-tilt five days a week and play in those two games the last two weeks of October, only to dodge the bullet that would finally hit him on November 5th.

Box 3.1. Of Gladiators and Goof Balls

"It is one of the blessings of old friends that you can afford to be stupid with them."

—Ralph Waldo Emerson

Seated underneath a green metal gazebo in our back yard on Elisa Drive, Preston is enjoying some down time after football practice with some of his fellow teammates. It is a very hot and humid afternoon in late August 2005, and he is 19 years old home for the weekend. Clothed in an old shabby green tee shirt, ragged around the arms from where he ripped the sleeves off, paired with light gray nylon gym shorts that sit low on his hips, rudely displaying his old dingy boxers. This nauseating trend of the saggy pants is something I will never understand. I suppose it is to be cool, masculine and bad-boyish, or maybe these boys just need to air their butt and nuts! I recall having heard that expression somewhere, but to me it seemed, at minimum, the most borderline logical reason available for this expression of ridiculousness, and I honestly could not think of any other explanation. Sitting inconspicuously over in the corner is Perry, a couple years younger than his brother, home from his job as a restaurant bus boy, quietly, inconspicuously, attempting to fit in with the older boys. Perry is different from Preston, much smaller in size, svelte, smart, and exceptionally shy, especially with the girls. Equally as athletic as Preston, he was simply not gifted with the same physical stature as his sibling, which would be his Achilles heel during these tender years. His sky-blue eyes so mesmerizing that you can find yourself lost in his soul if you are not careful.

Ah, such a delightfully magical portrait of young men, no longer children but not adults quite yet just passing the time away on this lazy hot summer day as I secretively stare out the kitchen window. I smile and say as I return to wiping down the counter, "Thank you Lord, all is well."

Suddenly there emerges a thunderous laughter amongst the boys that draw my attention back to the window as I peer out, leaning closer to the glass but still attempting not to blow my cover. If they should see me, Preston and Perry will denounce me as a spy, which will lead later on to the inevitable argument over the trust they believe they deserve as "young adults." Leaning so far back in his chair that only the two back legs are left on the ground (me wondering if those two legs of that bargain-basement lawn chair are rated to carry 225 pounds of strapping youth!), Preston's boisterous laughter bellows so intensely that I think for sure he is going to tip over.

What could be so funny? I wondered.

Then from the corner of my eye a frantic form emerges, Preston's friend John running wildly about the yard bearing an expression of utter panic, his face the color of a ruby red grapefruit, his arms flailing in a motion reminiscent of a bird desperately fleeing imminent danger. *Hmmm, maybe its bees; I'd seen a couple of carpenter bees flying around the house lately,* I think to myself. Yet strangely, rather than run to their friend's aid, the other boys seem to be finding this demonstration of dire distress hysterical as their remorseless laughing only escalates. Now Bob, another of Preston's friends shoots up, knocking over his chair, bending over and hugging his stomach, I can't tell if he is in pain or just laughing intensely at John. The obvious glee is uncontainable amongst the group.

What could be so funny? I wonder, more perplexed than ever. Yet I find myself falling into this contagious trap of laugher just looking at this absurd scene from a Fellini movie. I debate whether I should go out there to investigate further.

"Oh, these high-spirited teens are just thoughtless young animals as mettlesome as mosquitoes looking for their next meal," I say to myself as I walk over to the refrigerator to retrieve some cool lemonade for the boys on this hot August day. A clever ruse, perhaps, to venture outside? Little did I know just how hot things were about to become.

At that very moment, the kitchen door blasts open and Bill, another of Preston's friends, rushes in screaming, "My eyes, my eyes!" I run over to him and ask, "What's the matter?" as I try desperately to stay calm and cool for both our sakes. "My eyes are burning!" he cries in a tormented plea for help. I immediately grab his arms and rush him over to the sink.

"What happened?" I ask frantically; while grasping the back of his neck firmly I lower his head into the sink and with my other hand begin rinsing his eyes with the sink sprayer.

"Bill, why are your eyes burning?" I ask again, somewhat frustrated with his apparent incapacity to respond, while trying not to panic myself. Abruptly, the kitchen door explodes open again as Preston now comes bolting into the kitchen desperately looking for something cold to drink from the refrigerator.

My instinctual suspicions begin to rise as I turn to Preston and demand sternly; "Somebody better tell me what is going on here!" as I continue administering cold water to the stricken Bill. Preston wipes his mouth with the body of his shirt after drinking copiously from the milk carton and breathlessly blurts out, "Well, we had a bet to see who could withstand the challenge."

"What challenge? What are you talking about?" I'm almost stammering my words as I hand Bill a towel to wipe his now wet, red, and swollen eyes. He is still moaning in agony as he now rests his head in the towel cupped in both hands and rubbing his eyes. Preston continues to explain between generous gulps of the rest of the milk.

"Each of us had to take a big bite of a Habanero pepper we got from your garden, we had to chew it for 30 seconds, and then wait one minute before taking a drink of anything."

"What!" I exclaimed in disbelief, and beyond that I was too incredulous to think of anything else to say at that moment. OMG! That would explain why these nutty boys were thrashing about like people on fire!

I turn to Bill and ask, "Are you okay? Should I call your mom?"

"Please don't!" Bill pleads. "I'm okay. This was just stupid," he adds, his embarrassment so transparent that I decide to spare him the shameful ignominy of the call, as he lays his face back into the damp towel.

"Why do you teenagers seem to suddenly lose any resemblance of reasonable judgment and do such daffy things?" I ask, more a rhetorical lament than a question aimed at a constructive answer.

Just then Perry the younger comes waltzing in, blithely unscathed, having had the clever sense to pass on the challenge. I'm not surprised; he is the smart one. Shortly thereafter, John and Bob stumble into the kitchen, mildly exhibiting some of the tongue and esophageal scorching heat left lingering in their mouths and stomachs.

With the crisis over, I told the boys to sit down at the kitchen table and I will get them something to eat and drink. But the most remarkable thing happened, they began to laugh again, this time they were laughing at themselves, at their own stupidity and the foolishness of the challenge. *These boys are going to be alright*, I thought to myself. Preston, John and Bob had quite irrationally tried to run away from the intensity of the heat, and Bill had done the unfortunate escalating deed of rubbing his eyes with his hands infused with habanero oil, even after he ate this little orange pepper from hell. Lessons learned.

I chuckled to myself. "You know boys," I said as I walked over to the table and lay my hand on Bill's shoulder, "I've heard it said before that life is NOT like a box of chocolates, it's more like a garden of hot peppers. What you do today may burn your ass tomorrow."

CHAPTER 4

THE SECOND HIT

By all accounts, it was a perfectly legal hit. A vicious, full-tilt, perfectly legal hit.

In the waning minutes of the final quarter, Preston was called upon to play on special teams defending against a Duquesne punt return. Preston's uncanny eye for zeroing in on wherever the ball was made him a formidable and fearsome defender in what is arguably the most dangerous facet of the game. As the ball carrier attempted to dart past him, Preston turned downfield stalking the runner to make a tackle, his mind, body and soul riveted on chasing the ball, when he was hit solidly full-on in the chest and shoulder by an opposing blocker.

The hit was so forceful that it lifted my 225-pound linebacker son right off his feet—he was "de-cleated," as La Salle defensive line coach Petitte described it, meaning literally that his football cleats went airborne. Coach Petitte had a bird's eye view from along the sideline near the 35-yard marker where the violent collision occurred, so spectacular—and so loud the report—that from his vantage point, Petitte could see the gasping, breathless reaction of the mouths-agape players and fans of the opposing side directly across the field from him, as if they all felt the brutal force of the blow in their own chests. Preston's head rocketed immediately forward and then recoiled backwards as he flew hard to the turf.

Yet, while it was a terrifically hard shot to the body, there was no helmet-to-helmet contact and the opposing blocker had not deliberately left his own feet to try to spear Preston—a move that would indeed have been illegal—but rather, made the block with his shoulders and arms, turning his head and helmet away using proper form. In point of fact, he had done all the right things. And it was made at the full, lightning-fast speed that generally is only possible on punt and kickoff returns; ironically the very kind of magnificent hit that, had Preston somehow managed to get up and simply walk off the field, the announcers in the broadcast booth might very well have gleefully remarked with giddy excitement was "one for the highlight reel!" But Preston did not get up.

Instead, Preston was unconscious even before he hit the ground, where he lay limp and motionless for several seconds. Assistant Coach Petitte may have been the first person to get to Preston's side after the event; he remembered charging onto the field as soon as Preston went down, only hearing the referee's whistle blowing the play dead after he had started running out there. When he arrived, the vacant stare in Preston's eyes bore all of the extreme shock and electric apoplexy of a man who'd just been shot and was about to die. "I couldn't describe the look in his eyes," Petitte would later relate, in a sworn deposition. He grabbed a hold of Preston's hand and tried to get him to acknowledge.

Then just as abruptly, Preston exploded awake in a fury of agonizing pain and confusion and terror, his whole body and all his limbs convulsing uncontrollably. Some newspaper accounts would later describe Preston as "combative" when he awoke, but Coach Petitte—who had raced out onto the field ahead of LaSalle's Head Coach, LaSufe and several others in their efforts to try to attend to Preston—Coach Petitte knew better. Because when consciousness briefly returned, my boy began desperately screaming at him to do something to stop the excruciating pain in his head.

"He was down at first and then he tried to get up," Petitte said. "He started hollering about his head hurting and the pressure…. He said he felt the pressure in his head."

Preston tried desperately to stand up, to get back on his feet.

"We tried to restrain him so that the doctor could examine him," Petitte explained. "Because he wanted to get up and run away; it was like he was trying to get up and run away from all that pain he was talking about." But I know my son Preston, I believe he knew something was very wrong and didn't want to die, he wanted to live; he was only 19 years old. I believe that fiercely regaining consciousness for these few precious moments was my son's gallant attempt to get help and stay alive! Preston had an inner soul like a warrior, so strong, so tough, he was literally fighting for his life!

Almost immediately, however, Preston fell back down to his knees, his helmet and right shoulder dropping to the ground. He began foaming at the mouth, and less than a minute later, and as the contortions of his body started to subside, he became unresponsive once again as he began lapsing inexorably into a coma. Preston would later tell me about the near-death experience that he had at this very moment, which I will discuss later in this book.

It's an anguishing scene I shall always picture with utterly surreal clarity in my head even though I wasn't there to witness it myself; my beautiful boy down there on the ground in dire traumatic pain pleading for help that absolutely no one could give him at that moment, literally trying to run away, as if running could have helped him to escape the cruel severity of the pain. The sheer wincing, writhing, unrelenting pain my son must have experienced, and which must have been utterly unspeakable in words. And when the convulsions finally stopped and he lapsed into a coma, perhaps that was the only merciful thing that could happen at that moment.

Inside the stadium, the scene that played out before the scores of football fans in the aftermath of the horrendous hit—of nearly a dozen people, doctors and coaches and trainers and assistants all desperately huddled around Preston trying to help him but utterly helpless in their efforts—was so horrific that game officials and the coaches of both teams decided to end the game right then and there. There were only 2 minutes 42 seconds left on the game clock; minutes that would never be played, and the home team was leading by another lopsided, fait accompli score of 56 to 14. "Hard to go play football after you see something that," one of the local TV broadcasters said.

Not being there at the stadium that day to witness my son suffer such a catastrophic injury down on that merciless field of battle heartlessly trying to rob a warrior's soul of his existence was perhaps more than likely a good thing for me. To experience such a high degree of emotional distress from witnessing this calamitous vision would have played over and over again in my mind and highjack every thought and memory of him.

Preston was placed very carefully on a gurney, as it was believed at the time that my son may have suffered a spinal injury as well, and he was loaded into a waiting ambulance in which he was whisked immediately to Mercy Hospital located only two blocks away from Duquesne's football stadium—a factor that may have saved Preston's life. Coach Petitte rode in the ambulance with Preston still holding on tightly to his hand, squeezing if from time to time and taking what little optimism he could muster from the fact that, on occasion, while cognitively he was completely out, it seemed to Petitte that Preston occasionally squeezed back. Unfortunately, however, this squeeze of the hand that Coach Petitte wanted to believe was a good sign was in all likelihood a phenomenon known as the Palmar Grasp Reflex. The Palmar Grasp Reflex is a primitive reflex usually associated with infants, but it is also very common in connection with many cases of coma. Regrettably, while the reflex is quite normal in infants, in whom it is believed to be a vestigial phenomenon from our primate ancestors, who's young needed to be able to grasp onto their mother's fur for protection and survival, it is not a good sign in adults who suffer severe brain damage.

The driver of the ambulance careened the vehicle over sidewalks as he raced to get to the ER entrance as fast as he possibly could. Meanwhile the Head Coach and LaSufe sprinted down the city streets from the field to the hospital.

As the paramedics rushed Preston's gurney through the emergency room doors, an ER nurse carrying emergency room instruments in her arms immediately recognized the urgency and severity of Preston's injury and literally dropped everything, the metal instruments clanging down onto the floor. She then quickly prioritized Preston over a gunshot victim who had also just come into the hospital. In another coincidence that may have ultimately saved my son's life, neurosurgeons Eric Altschuler and Daniel Bursick were at that very moment finishing up a surgical procedure in one of Mercy Hospitals operating rooms, when they got the call that there was an incoming patient with severe head trauma. Dr. Altschuler quite literally threaded his last stitch to close the incision, ordered the operating room to be prepped for a possible emergency, snapped off his surgical gloves and rushed down to the ER admitting area.

As soon as he saw Preston he noticed instantly that his right eye was dilated and fixed and he was exhibiting decerebrate posturing, which is an indicator of an acute brain injury, so he ordered that my son be brought into the OR immediately. Altschuler believed that Preston had only minutes to live, and there was absolutely no time to lose. Recognizing the sheer enormity of the injury, Dr. Bursick agreed to stay and assist Dr. Altschuler, and the first thing the two neurosurgeons did was to perform a frontotemporal-parietal craniotomy—which is to say that Altschuler removed practically the entire top right side of Preston's skull—as the only means available to relieve the extreme pressure caused by life-threatening swelling of the brain. They then removed a massive subdural hematoma, or blood clot, and for the next several hours, the two doctors struggled to staunch the massive and uncontrolled bleeding from arteries in the tissues surrounding Preston's brain.

* * * * *

November 5th, 2005 was a cool and windy day back home in our town of Marlboro, New Jersey and the Marlboro High School Mustang football game had just wrapped up, resulting in another disappointing loss for the home team. The outcome aside, it was an important game nonetheless, because it was the annual Parent's Day game, the one at which the graduating senior players are honored, playing in their final season, as well as their parents thanked for supporting both the players and the football program itself. Perry was one of the graduating seniors.

Football was always a very big part of our lives. As parents of our time, it was very common not only to have our kids actively participate in school sports but also in organized sports outside the school in our community. Both my boys, Preston and Perry, had played numerous sports since they were very young, from our local Pop Warner Football League as well as Little League Baseball, and all the way up through to high school. Throughout these years, Ted, who himself had played semi-pro football in Brooklyn back in his early 20s, coached our boys in both football and baseball, while over the majority of that time I was a "team mother" as well as a member of the Pop Warner Trustees. Both boys also participated in soccer, basketball, and even Taekwondo. However, when they reached high school I helped develop and implement the Marlboro High School Mustang Football Parents Club and became very active in all of its functions. I found myself so absorbed in the affairs of this club that I cannot really say that I ever actually watched a complete home game, as I attended to all of the side attractions and fundraisers sponsored or hosted by the Parents Club.

In any case, in the opening ceremony to the Parent's Day game, we were given the privilege of walking Perry in uniform across the field to the cheers of the crowd, and while I might have appreciated that gesture, to me and to Ted it was really Perry's day to be recognized for his hard work and effort, and his athletic performance on the field. Perry did not possess the physical size and power of Preston but his cunningness and quickness on the field was equally as impressive. While the festivities of the day began on a high note unfortunately would end on a low note with another loss. After the game the boys had all gone into the locker room to change out of their uniforms, shower, and get dressed in their street clothes.

I was your typical football mom—no different than all of the other moms that day, as we huddled in one group near the field trying to figure out what words of wisdom to say to the boys, after another loss, when they would finally emerge from the locker room. Probably something foolish like, *I feel your pain and sympathize with you over your loss*, or in my case I might even have tried to do the thing that is so hideously unimaginable to a teenage boy: Stretch out my arms to give a comforting mother's hug. Yikes! You can imagine how well that would go over right in front of all their teammates. So, the hugs always waited until we got home and out of sight.

If alternatively, you told the boys, "good effort," they would look at you strangely and then lower and shake their heads in stupefaction. One would think that after all these years as a team mom at every game I would come to understand the hard way they took the losses, but I never did, and the plain truth was that I was crushed just as much as they were every time. It's only a game, people say, but it was ever so important to them.

I loved this game of football at the time, but it was becoming more difficult to find the right words to comfort them because they had gone through a string of losses that season. I found that saying nothing was perhaps the best way to go, and to just let them come to you if they wanted to talk about it. They were feeling bad enough and did not need to talk about how bad they played when they had practiced so hard all through the preceding week. Of course, Ted and the other dads were over by the fence second-guessing the play calling the coaches had employed to ultimately lose the game. That's what dads do, I guess. These boys were so tired of practicing so hard only to lose just about every game this season. For our part, Ted and I had been through this same scenario before when Preston attended Marlboro High School two years earlier, when he also experienced four years of losing seasons. Yes, I would have to say it was a very tough season for Perry back in 2005 and what made it worse was that it was his senior year and, sad to say, his fourth year of a losing season. While that may be devastating for a competitive-minded 17 year-old senior, in hindsight I wish I could say that lack of victory on the football field would have been Preston's only problem.

As we waited outside the school gym for the boys to come out, Ted and I were anticipating Preston's usual Saturday afternoon phone call to report the outcome of his game. Of course, we were very consciously aware that Preston was playing 350 miles away in Pittsburgh, where the LaSalle Explorers were duking it out with the Duquesne University Dukes. I was standing with a few of the mothers and we were just chatting about Perry's game, when I noticed some distance away that Ted had moved over to a quiet corner of the grounds, where he was standing alone, talking on his cell phone. "Oh, Ted must be on the phone with Preston. I wonder if he lost his game too." I said it jokingly to the other mothers, followed with a kind of a snickering and sarcastic smirk. As I've said, neither the Marlboro High School or the La Salle University football programs were ones that fostered a great deal of optimism or abundant expectations of victory on the gridiron.

Just then Ted turned my way and his eyes met mine for just an instant. He had no smile, his face appeared sullen and grim, and he began to trudge slowly over to me, like a man carrying a heavy weight on his shoulders. I asked somewhat cynically; "Well, did Preston lose his game too?" He looked at me with utter fear and urgency in his eyes. "We need to get to Pittsburgh as soon as possible," he said, "Preston is at the hospital in the operating room undergoing brain surgery." I stared at him for a moment in disbelief, but his expression remained rigid as he stared back at me, stone-faced, serious.

"What? Is this some sort of joke?" I asked.

Now, if that question sounds odd to you, well, life is full of cruel ironies. Only a week earlier, as Ted and I were asleep in bed, we had been awakened by a phone call somewhere between midnight and one in the morning. Ted had been the one to get up to answer it, and when he did, he uttered barely two words. "Oh, okay."

That was all he said into the receiver, and then he promptly hung up.

"Who was that? I asked.

Ted responded groggily yet expressing a serious voice, "Well, we have to get up and go to Philly. That was the police. Apparently, Preston's been arrested for possession of drugs and he's in some sort of trouble."

I got up and we both started to get dressed, but the more I thought about this, the weirder it seemed to me; something was just not right. I began grilling Ted about the call. What had the caller said? What sort of trouble was Preston in? Was it drugs or drinking? What was he being charged with? Was he being held in jail somewhere? My mind was spinning with dozens of questions that Ted had not even thought to ask the caller—questions that frankly, I would have asked had I been the one who picked up the phone.

So of course, Ted had no answers whatsoever. He could not even say if the call had come from the campus police or from the Philadelphia city police force. "I don't know, I don't know," he kept saying, as if annoyed and feeling tormented by my unrelenting barrage of questions. "We just have to get dressed," Ted retorted, "The detective said he would call us back in a few minutes with more details and instructions about where to go."

Now this was really inexplicably odd, and I was simply dumbfounded. Why couldn't this "detective" have given Ted all of that information when he had my husband on the phone to begin with? What detective? What was his name? Even though it has always been my nature to be somewhat suspicious of issues regarding my rambunctious and sometimes mischievous boys, this call just did not sound right. Yet despite all of it, as two dutiful parents wanting to do the right thing we sat like a couple of lumps in the family room waiting for this follow-up call to come through. Finally, after about five minutes of this nonsense, I'd had enough. "I'm not waiting; I'm going to call them back," I said.

Ted said, "I don't have the number."

That's when I hit upon the idea of checking the caller ID on the land line. It read, "Private number." Now I knew for certain that something was categorically wrong with this whole fiasco. So I looked up the number for the La Salle Campus Police department and called them directly. The dispatcher told me that there had been no incidents on campus that evening that they knew about, involving Preston or anyone else for that matter, nor were they holding anyone at the moment for possession of drugs. And indeed, the dispatcher confirmed my suspicion when he suggested that we had been the victims of a prank call.

Still, in an excess of motherly caution, I asked to have an officer go over to Preston's residence, which was just off campus, to check on him and make sure everything was okay. Less than ten minutes later, we got a call from our confused and bewildered son, who was clearly still groggy from having been asleep, asking us why in the world we had called the police on him.

Now, most people, those with a good sense of humor at least, love and enjoy a good prank, even when it is played on them. In the scheme of things, however, I didn't think this qualified as a "good" or "funny" prank whatsoever; quite to the contrary I thought it was a particularly un-funny and disturbing one, even mean-spirited, only made worse by the ironic coincidence that it happened to come at a most inopportune moment in our lives. We never did find out who made that foolish and distressing call. At this point, I don't really want to know.

And so, on that afternoon a week later, standing outside Marlboro High School, when I asked if he was joking, Ted looked at me with serious and unflinching solemnity in his face.

"Why would I joke about such a thing?" he said.

Perhaps I should have realized immediately. Because, in all the years that I had known Ted, I had never before seen him this way. He was anxious and confused, clearly upset, and his demeanor displayed such urgency to get to Preston that I came to realized that this was no joke and we had a very serious situation on our hands.

The only way I can describe what happened to me from that moment on was that I entered some sort of cognitive, emotional, perceptual bubble; I was single-mindedly focused on only one thing; getting to Pittsburgh as quickly as humanly possible; on getting to Preston by any means necessary. If I could have willed myself to be mystically transported through time and space to be by his side now, this very moment, I would have done that. At the same time, the rest of my reality seemed to fade into oblivion; suddenly the facts and circumstances of the passing moments would no longer compute in the logical and rational way they are supposed to.

Where did Ted suddenly disappear to? (I had actually forgotten, almost instantly as the words came out of his mouth, that he had told me he was going to get the car.)

What was I doing here? (I was supposed to be waiting to collect Perry the moment he emerged from the locker room.)

I did not know what to do other than I just needed to get to Preston. My mind was trying to process all the emotions I was feeling and I was finding it difficult, and crushingly so, because there were so many thoughts circling absurdly and uncontrollably in my head, so I must have forgotten all about Perry at that instant and I just started to walk. As if trying to get *somewhere*. My scope of vision was a blur and the deafening sound of my own heart breaking from pounding so intensely was all I could hear in my head. Adrift in that bubble of isolation I gasped for air as I tried to breathe in, breathe out, desperately trying to rein control my emotions, my thoughts, my sense of rationality. I felt so utterly alone. I hadn't even realized exactly when I had begun to cry.

Where was Ted, where was Perry? I feel so alone. We've got to get to the hospital; we've got to get to Pittsburgh. Now.

Somehow, I found myself at the back of the school where the door to the locker room was located. That's where I saw Don, one of Perry's teammates just as he happened to come out through the door. I beckoned to him with such intensity and distressed tears asking him to please go find Perry for me immediately and tell him to hurry; tell him that there was an emergency at home. As one of Perry's best friends and a frequent visitor to our home, Don knew me well enough to recognize my sheer terror and to realize that something truly was very wrong. He did not ask questions, he just turned and high-tailed like a true Mustang in flight back into the building to find Perry.

Where was Ted? My mind turned again to the whereabouts of my now missing-in-action husband. Because he had dropped me off at the front of the school when we first arrived for the day's festivities, I had no idea where he has parked the car, and no idea where to look for it. Urgency without any definitive direction raced throughout my dazed and distraught mind, such that I resumed my mindless walking, zombie-like I suppose, through the now nearly empty parking lot, trying, almost insanely, to get to Preston. My motherly mentality commanded just one thought and that was to get to Preston even if I had to run to wherever he was. I didn't know where anyone else was; where was Ted, where was Perry, and where exactly at this moment was my suffering boy Preston? My heart ached with the excruciating knowledge that he was all alone and so far away, none of his family there to comfort him. *He must be so scared*, I anguished. I had to get to him. And as I trudged on, locked in this bubble of transfixed emotions, I started to do the only rational thing my mind could muster; I started to walk home. Just then the sound of a far-a-way voice begins to penetrate into my world of distress when a car pulled up alongside of me and a familiar voice rupturing my self-inflicted emotional daze.

"Mom? What's wrong? Where are you going?"

It was Perry, driving home in his old grey and tattered Hyundai Elantra raked out to suit the racecar-like preferences of a teenager, along with another of his teammates, his good friend Chuck, who was riding in the front passenger seat. Fortunately, Perry had spotted me walking alone and distraught in the parking lot just as he was proceeded to the exit. I don't know if Don had ever found him in the locker room, but my distress seemed to be wholly and unequivocally apparent to my second son.

I threw open the rear door and jumped into the back seat.

"Preston is hurt really bad and we need to get him right away," I blurted.

Those were the only words I could find it in my power to say; it was exhausting just to utter them. And for the remainder of the drive home, I simply lowered my head and started to recite the Lord's Prayer softly, over and over, each word pleading for grace amid the tears flowing down my distraught face. There was not another sound in the car beyond the cyclone of wind blowing through the open windows and carrying—I remember hoping with all my heart—each and every word of my prayers up to the heavens. Perry would not speak a word during the entire trip home, driving with a look of sober determination on his face, yet too young and too confused to fully understand the gravity of the situation. Or maybe during this car trip home his silence simply meant I was just embarrassing him in front of his friend. It's hard to say which it might have been.

When we got home, Ted was still missing (in my hyper-frantic mind, at least), much to my ever-increasing consternation. Never mind that I had in fact unwittingly abandoned him, and he'd probably spent precious urgent minutes at the school searching for me after he'd retrieved the car. Perry started to ask questions and as I explained to him what was happening we just held each other and cried. "Preston is tough," Perry suddenly asserted, assuring me that all of this was probably nothing, that Preston would more than likely be just fine, that there was absolutely nothing that would keep his big brother down. However, while I may have not seen it at the time, this emotional declaration would turn out to be a poignant sign of things to come, including a gathering measure of denial on Perry's part.

And with all that Preston had been through in his football playing life, all those years where he was the undisputed best player on bad teams and as a direct consequence the prime target of the most vicious hits, yet had come through virtually every game unscathed with a huge smile on his face, it had made perfect sense for Perry to say all of those positive things. I had wanted with all my heart to believe him. Yet at the same time, this was one of the only moments, however brief, that I can honestly say I ever saw any shedding of tears coming from Perry. He was trying to be optimistic and strong with his words, but fell weak to the throes of his emotions.

With Ted still not at home— *"Where is that man??!!"* I recall exclaiming with angry exasperation through my gritted teeth and rolling tears—although I did have enough mental where-with-all to reason that he probably knew that I had come home in Perry's car, since when parted I had told him that I would get Perry as soon as he came out of the locker room, and that Ted no doubt would be home shortly. Nevertheless, I took the bull by the horns and got on the phone to try to get a flight for all three of us from Newark to Pittsburgh. I was mortified to find that everything was booked on such short notice. Just then Ted finally walked in the door and I told him there were no flights and that we all needed to just get in the car and go. I did not even question where he had been all this time—it no longer mattered—nor did I want to waste another minute.

"Let's just go!" I shouted. And with that the three of us piled into the car with nothing more than our worries, fears and tears, Ted behind the wheel and gunning the vehicle headlong towards Pittsburgh, a six-hour car ride from our home.

We had barely gotten onto the southbound barrel of the NJ Turnpike when we got a call from Herb, the father of another one of Perry's good friends and fellow football teammate. Word about Preston was spreading like wildfire all over our town, and this may have provided a clue as to the reason why I had lost track of Ted for all of those agonizing moments between the high school and home. Because when my caring and concerned husband becomes upset or worried, he talks—and he talks *a lot*. As you might imagine from the kind of kid Preston was, he had left his mark on the Marlboro High School football program as well as the entire school community itself, and pretty soon a lot of people in our community were concerned and pulling and praying for him.

I explained to Herb that there were no flights from Newark so we were just driving to get there. That's when he said, "Did you try the Philadelphia airport?"

Oh My God! I exclaimed; *the Philadelphia airport!*

In my single-minded, precision-missile-strike determination to get to Pittsburgh as soon as humanly possible, I had completely overlooked this obvious alternative, and yet here we were already headed in the exact direction we needed to get there! I kindly thanked Herb and abruptly ended the call with him and then searched and immediately dialed up the Philadelphia airport. By the grace and goodness of God there was a flight to Pittsburgh, scheduled to depart in just a scant hour, and which miraculously could accommodate all three of us. This to me was beyond amazing, because it would mean that we would be able to board the flight just as soon as we arrived—there would be no waiting around in anguished, pacing, hand-wringing helplessness. Had it come to that, I seriously think I'd have just about lost my sanity completely.

At the same time, however, we were cutting it razor-close to even getting there in time to make the flight—God forbid there should be an accident or a traffic jam at any point along the way. This was New Jersey, after all, a state that is famously a motorist's nightmare, and the labyrinth of roads leading into Philadelphia International was certainly no better. At that point I willed that no power on Earth was going to prevent us from getting on that big, beautiful plane and get to our stricken boy, and for once, the highways mercifully cooperated.

Still, when we arrived at the airport parking lot we were enormously pressed for time if we were going to make our flight. Amazingly, just as we were getting out of the car, I spotted a shuttle making its way to the bus stop— the stop was not too far away but I realized we were still going to have to make a run for it, and I was bound and determined that we were going to be on *this* shuttle. I mean, who knew how long it might be until the next one would come ambling along?

I started to walk fast with my sight totally fixated on making that shuttle, waving my arms to the driver to make damn sure he saw me. I was relieved when I saw him nod his head, smiling warmly and waving back. Upon reaching the shuttle stop, I suddenly realized that I had far outpaced Ted and Perry in getting there, and I confess that it was not without some inner nagging annoyance over the fact that Ted just did not seem to share my acute sense of extreme white-knuckles urgency in this catastrophic situation. Or so I thought for the fleeting moment.

Because when I turned to yell "Come on you guys, hurry!" I discovered to my horror that Perry was bent over double, vomiting in the street by a lamppost, with Ted standing protectively at his side, appearing to have a comforting hand resting on Perry's shoulder. Little did I know at the time that this comforting hand on Perry's shoulder was only there to aide in his balance—and to block anyone's view—as he subsequently relieved himself in the airport parking lot. My poor husband: in our rush to get out of the house, and in his not wanting to risk stopping at an NJ Turnpike rest area lest we miss our flight, who knows how long that poor man had needed to go!

Regardless of course, all I could think at that moment was: *This can't be happening, we are going to miss this shuttle! We are going to miss the plane!* May I ever be forgiven for these, the immediate and immutable thoughts that lit up my mind upon seeing my second son getting violently sick in an airport parking lot?

All I kept thinking was we needed to get to Preston; I'd not given the least bit of consideration to what Perry must be going through. This was his blood brother, his best friend and his athletic comrade-in-arms, who was in serious trouble. It was not some distant family member or friend, but a brother with whom he had a very special bond and, I believe, a uniquely close relationship as brothers go. They both had a high respect for each other, and even if they occasionally had their spats, like all siblings do, they always got along together remarkably. How could I have failed to see that the emotional rollercoaster ride of this horrific and ever-widening trauma was affecting him, not just psychologically and emotionally, but even downright physically to the point of actually making him sick to his stomach?

And yet I well knew that Perry was never one to commonly show his emotions outwardly very often, if at all. Yet here, however, this intensely painful drama had immersed itself so deeply into every nerve of his body that his inner anguish and tension was forced to be physically discharged with abounding fury… in the middle of the street. In my fixation on getting to Preston, I had been utterly blind to it all, and when I look back on these events today, I have such regret and guilt that I did not attend to Perry's emotional well-being in a more thoughtful and motherly way. All it would have taken from me was to give him a loving hug or a smile that said everything is going to be all right. Somehow, I had lost sight of the fact that he was only 17 years old, and he was scared, too, even as he struggled bravely to show no fear. Of course, it was never my intention to give Perry the false impression that the awful pain he was feeling was by any measure less significant than mine or Ted's. I just wasn't thinking about all of that, because all that I was capable of thinking in those moments was, we had to get to Preston.

Just then the shuttle bus pulled up to the stop, and as soon as the doors hissed open I leaned in and begged the driver to wait for the others. From his perch up in the driver's seat he looked down at me, and he must have observed my red and swollen eyes, the fact that I was still crying. He saw Perry in dire distress, sick and upset in the street, Ted standing with him and looking help-lessly apologetic, and I believe he understood that something was very wrong here. I'll never forget the compassion this man showed by waiting until we were all at last ready to press on. Once again the heavens seemed to have smiled upon us, or maybe just took pity, as I realized there were no other passengers already in the shuttle, nor were there any other people boarding at this stop besides the three of us. Even further, as soon as we were underway, I'm pretty sure that benevolent driver broke all of the speed limits in whisking us right over to the terminal entrance without a moment's delay.

Anxiously processing at the ticket counter, we received another call. This time it was LaSalle's Coach, calling to update us on Preston's status. The good news was that by this time, our son was out of surgery; however, he was now in the ICU Trauma Unit in critical condition. The Coach respectfully explained that he preferred not to go into any of the specific details over the phone, promising to tell us everything as soon as we got there. I vaguely recollect that he then proceeded to try to give me some specific instructions for what we needed to do as soon as we touched down in the Steel City, but it was as if I was hearing some distracting voice blaring away in the back of my head, and I simply could not fully comprehend what he was saying any more. In fact, I felt detached and oblivious to everything else around me for that matter, the car, the road, even my family members.

I kept thinking an endless unstoppable loop of uncontrollable, cascading, repeating thoughts, thinking about my boy. My head was tight like when you have a massive sinus attack, the very skin of my face feeling like it was constricting my features. All it seemed I could do was to listen without actually hearing; it was becoming increasingly difficult, even impossible for me to speak coherently. It was so odd; there was something inside me that no matter how hard I would try, pretty soon I could no longer talk at all; I simply could not get the words out. I just kept crying. So, I finally handed the phone over to Ted.

The Coach told Ted that they would have a car waiting to meet us at the airport and bring us to the hospital, after which, there being really nothing else to discuss, Ted said goodbye and clicked off the call. The ticketing agents did their best to get us processed quickly, and we would get to the gate with mere minutes to spare. Yet even that final sprint was not without a measure of post 9/11 high drama and suspense, courtesy of homeland security and the dutiful agents of the Homeland Security Administration (TSA).

You'd have thought that navigating through the security checkpoint would have been a breeze. After all, we had no luggage, no laptop computers or iPads, not even so much as a toothbrush among us, and the biggest non-clothing article we carried was my handbag.

However, when I got dressed that morning of November 5, 2005, it was beyond anyone's imagination that I would find myself running to catch an airplane flight. No, I had dressed for comfort in preparation for enjoying Marlboro High's annual Parents' Day event, and what was likely to be Perry's most well attended and most memorable game as a senior. And then suddenly, the scanners and blinking lights of the TSA X-ray booth quickly detected—and blared loudly the alert—that I was wearing an underwire bra. Really.

And so of course, I was pulled aside for, shall we say, a more "personal" screening. Naturally, my desperate from-the-heart pleas in trying to explain to the stone-faced, weary-eyed TSA agent in 25 words or less why it was so drop-dead critically important for me to be on that plane, my words nevertheless fell on unsympathetic ears; understandably perhaps, since he had undoubtedly heard that story a million times before. How could I expect him to understand?

Regardless, once the search was over, we ran like hell to get to the gate, and with the help of God, we made it onto the plane. And then, perhaps as a measure of celestial recompense (some good karma!), as we were preparing to take off the pilot came on the speaker to announce that we would be arriving in Pittsburgh a half hour earlier than expected. And to this day, no one may tell me that God was not at work on that awful day; a last-ditch phone call from a concerned and caring friend about an airport, a compassionate shuttle bus driver willing to break a few rules, and a hail-Mary ride on the wings of angels providing a flight-shortened ETA. Yet even as I settled into my seat in coach, I could not stop the tears.

As ought to be pretty clear by now, my husband Ted is not one for high drama or tragedy. And frankly, it isn't just that he is not interested in occurrences or events that present with high dramatic impact or enormous stress—he manifestly disdains such occurrences or events, and when life's inevitable dramas do come up, he does everything in his power to avoid them. When pushed, however he purposely positions psychological distance by utilizing, some would say, "tasteless humor"—often quite effectively I might add—bizarre declarations or jokes that I call *Tedism's*—thus leaving me to handle some of our most challenging situations completely alone. Despite being so unfair and strenuous on me, in some ways I suppose, it is this coping mechanism that nevertheless can render him a steady and even rational rock through the hard times we were facing at that moment, and the ones that were yet to come.

Whatever the case, I have to acknowledge that Ted was certainly not relishing the prospect of being forced to sit next to me listening to me quietly whimpering over the course of this entire flight to Pittsburgh. In point of fact,

Ted does not like to fly in the first place, so he was already uncomfortable the moment he stepped nervously into the cabin of the plane. But at the last moment, just as the pilot spun the nose of the plane to point down the runway, and just before the engines began to rev up, Ted turned to me and Perry and—right on cue—said with a devilish grin, "Hey, wouldn't it be funny if the plane goes down in flames and we all perish and then Preston wakes up perfectly fine only to learn that we're all dead?!"

CHAPTER 5

SAVING PRESTON

"People pay the doctor for his trouble; for his kindness they still remain in his debt."

—Seneca (4 B.C. - 65 A.D.)

When Preston arrived in the ER at Mercy Hospital, he was immediately given a CT scan. Dr. Altschuler took one look at the scan and said to the nurses on duty, "Get him in the OR. We've got to do this now." In the scan he had seen a massive pan hemispheric subdural hematoma with brain herniation, so large in fact that the neurologist fully anticipated that he would find numerous other complications once he got to work. Preston was comatose and unresponsive to any commands; he was frothing at the mouth, and he had what medical people commonly refer to as a blown pupil. A "blown pupil" is a pupil that is dilated, meaning that it is large and fixed, and does not respond to a shining light; it is perilous, a life-threatening indicator of brain herniation, meaning that there was massive brain swelling and pressure building inside the skull that needed to be relieved immediately or Preston would die. Preston was also experiencing bouts of decerebrate posturing, a kind of full-body spasmodic seizure that is the result of severe damage to the primordial part of the brain, the amygdala, commonly referred to as the brain stem.

Simply described, decerebrate posturing is an abnormal posture in which the arms and legs are held straight out and down toward the sides of the body, the head and neck arched tautly back, and the toes of the feet pointed downward. In this state, all of the muscles in Preston's body became intensely tightened and held rigidly. It is a patterned movement through which the body reacts to extremely painful stimuli when the thinking part of the brain is not working, but only the primitive part, which is the brain stem. Decerebrate posturing earns a life-threatening score of 1 or 2 on the 6-point motor component of the Glasgow Coma Scale (in which low scores are the most severe). Here I must tell you that decerebrate posturing is a terrifying thing to witness, particularly when you see it happening to your own son right in front of you, and it's even more horribly anguishing when you learn that it's an indicator that he is experiencing severe pain even though he is comatose, unresponsive, and can't even call out for help! I know this because we would later witness a frightening episode of this reaction within only an hour or so after we would finally arrive at Preston's bed side. But this was only the beginning of his medically expanding ordeal.

While the following information may seem a bit tricky in understanding some of the medical terms, I feel that it is important to detail the massive amount of significant damage done to Preston's brain as well as any complications to remind you that all this immense dire destruction was from the cost of playing football.

Preston had also suffered a posterior cerebral artery infarction, which is a stroke that occurs in patients who have such severe brain swelling that, as extreme pressure builds rapidly inside the skull, the brain essentially starts to look for places to go. It obviously can't go out through the skull itself, and therefore the only available place it can expand is through the opening in the base of the skull, known as the foramen magnum, where the brain connects to the spinal cord. Critically however, as the brain starts herniating to that spot, it literally kinks off like a garden hose the blood vessels that live there, which creates a major stroke and possible death. One of the most common blood vessels it kinks off is the posterior cerebral artery. When that happens, the major stroke that results in turn creates further brain swelling, and a vicious cascading cycle quickly kicks into gear as the swelling kinks off other arteries throughout the brain and creates more strokes.

During the course of the surgical operation, Drs. Altschuler and Bursick would discover that Preston suffered numerous mini strokes among the web of arteries across the region at the top of the brain in addition to the posterior cerebral artery infarction at the brain stem. We would find out many years later that the radiologist who originally reviewed Preston's CT scan initially underestimated the size of Preston's hematoma as a moderate subdural rather than an extreme one, and he apparently altogether missed the equally severe stroke. Neurosurgeon Altschuler chose to be very diplomatic when he later stated for the record, "I'm not sure of the best way to say it, but I trust my interpretation of the images more than [the interpretation of the radiologist]," although he was bluntly unequivocal in acknowledging that the same radiologist, "missed the stroke that was there." This is why it is so imperative that a qualified neuro-radiologist reads CT brain scans, and that this critical task is not left to a regular radiologist.

Before he was even wheeled into the operating room, Preston was given a shot of Mannitol, a medicine formulated to reduce the swelling, and a breathing tube was inserted, in effect to help him to "over-breathe," as the doctor put it, to infuse more oxygen into his system. That's because studies have shown that if you can enhance a severe brain injury patient's breathing, you can reduce some of the swelling in the brain, at least temporarily. And then the first thing that Dr. Altschuler did in the operating room was to perform a frontotemporal-parietal craniotomy (FTP), which involved the removal of a large portion of Preston's skull—as the only means available to relieve the extreme pressure that was building within as a result of the massive brain swelling that was occurring.

Once the two neurosurgeons had removed what is commonly called the bone flap, which in Preston's case was practically the whole top right side of his skull, they found the dura—which is the layer of protective tissue that surrounds the brain—to be quite tense and under severe pressure, and they could also see the massive hematoma or blood clot below the dura, and that is also why it is called a subdural hematoma. However, the dura itself was also extremely swollen with fluid, mostly plasma, that Dr. Altschuler literally had to prick a hole in the dura layer with a scalpel so that whatever was causing it to bleed could be released, and also so that he could open the dura in order to remove the blood clot. When he did so, the dura gushed with fluid; in medical terms, this is referred to as "spontaneous exudation under severe high pressure [of] clear serous fluid." Dr. Altschuler would later explain to Ted and me that Preston had sustained such an acute and sudden shock to the brain that the plasma of the blood did not even have a chance to congeal to form a uniform clot. This would explain at least one reason why there was so much out-of-control bleeding.

In fact, because there was so much bleeding, Dr. Altschuler was very grateful that Dr. Bursick had agreed to stay and assist in the operation. Working together, the two doctors were better able to see the origins of numerous bleeds and to repair them. It may be useful here to understand that there are no arteries or veins within the brain itself. In nature's evolutionary effort to pack as much "gray matter" into the human brain, it eventually became the case that there was simply no room for these vessels. Instead, the brain's blood flow needs are served by a web of blood vessels that weave the surface of the brain much like a hair net. The way that blood drains from the brain in this complex system is that a network of miniscule veins drains into a very large vein— called the sagittal sinus and located in the middle part of the brain—via what are known as a cortical bridging veins; *bridging* because they connect the hair-net network of brain blood vessels to the primary vein (the sagittal sinus) which in turn carries the blood from the head down to the heart. In Preston's case, he experienced severe hemorrhaging from several of those bridging veins, though it is not known exactly how many bleeds there were; in their urgent rush to essentially seal off all of the bleeds, the two doctors had no time to waste by trying to count them.

Drs. Altschuler and Bursick used an instrument called a bipolar electrocautery machine to evacuate the fluid from subdural hematoma on the surface of the brain and to stop the numerous bleeds among the bridging veins. The way this machine works is that it enables the surgeon to seal off blood vessels by passing an electrical current between the tips of what looks like a pair of very elongated tweezers to create a tiny clot—a process called cauterizing—that stops the bleeding. (Think of the lightning-like bolt of visible electrical current passing between those strange operating lab contraptions in just about every Frankenstein horror film that's ever been made.) Typically, in these types of operations, one person uses a suction device to clear the fluids while the lead surgeon uses the cautery device for as long as 45 minutes to an hour to stop all of the bleed points.

Even further, however, Dr. Altschuler found that the surface of the top of Preston's brain was covered with numerous petechial hemorrhages. Petechial hemorrhages are essentially small contusions or bruises caused by the brain being violently bounced around like a tennis ball inside the skull cavity, a phenomenon Dr. Altschuler would later liken to a severe case of shaken baby syndrome. In effect, Preston's brain was battered all over with bruises from being shaken around inside his skull as a result of the violent impact on the field. The doctor's concern was that these brain bruises would continue to swell even after surgery, sometimes referred to as secondary swelling, which in Preston's case would continue to be severe, and it was just one of the reasons that led Dr. Altschuler ultimately to decide not to try to put the skull bone flap back in place when the brain operation itself was complete. (It is worth noting that these petechial hemorrhages or brain bruises cause scarring and hardening of the outer layers of the brain tissue and would later cause Preston to experience severe epileptic seizures, as I will describe later in this book.) Another reason for his decision, which I firmly believe was the right one, is that he inserted a tube into the water sac of Preston's brain in order to allow fluid to continue to drain as a means of controlling any further swelling. And as if all of Preston's brain injury issues weren't enough, he faced several other critical challenges to his immediate survival.

The first was that he suffered a punctured and collapsed lung, which likely occurred when the ER technicians rushed to insert the breathing tube prior to undergoing the neurosurgery. But he also quickly developed an E. Coli urinary tract infection, a strain of an influenza infection (known medically as Haemophilus influenzae) and a respiratory tract infection called Klebsiella tracheobronchitis. Ironically, all of these infections were likely contracted as Preston was being admitted to Mercy Hospital and may have occurred in connection with either his initial stabilizing treatment or in preparation for surgery. For example, the urinary tract infection may have resulted from the necessary insertion of a catheter, the respiratory infection may have come from the tracheotomy and insertion of the breathing tube that pierced his lung, and the influenza bug may have been transmitted through physical contact with a nurse or technician. And while all of these infections might have been minor in nature (and not particularly unusual in the case of any person being prepped for surgery as Preston had been), and would be easily controllable in the case of a normal person, each one of them posed potentially life-threatening danger to Preston because, in concentrating its efforts to deal with his severe brain injury, his body's immune system was now severely compromised.

That is in part because patients with severe brain injuries often suffer massive disruptions of the mechanisms that regulate their hormonal systems. In particular, the master hormonal regulatory gland known as the pituitary can sometimes be damaged in a head injury after herniation occurs. So, for example, one set of glands that the pituitary controls are the adrenal glands that produce the body's natural steroids. When the adrenal gland gets fouled up, the injured person can variously experience dangerous high- and low-blood pressure episodes, as well as sweating and high fever. In Preston's case, for example, for weeks after his surgery he would carry sweating fevers as frighteningly high as 104 degrees! In effect, when the pituitary gland is injured, all of the internal regulatory mechanisms that we take for granted can be severely compromised or disrupted with their own life-threatening consequences.

These formidable immunological concerns led Dr. Altschuler to make another important professional decision. In most cases in which a craniotomy is performed and where, for whatever reason, the decision is made to not put the bone flap back in place immediately upon completion of the internal surgical procedure, the flap itself is placed inside the patient's body. Basically, an incision is made, usually in the area of the abdomen, and a "pocket" is formed in which the bone flap is placed, literally for storage, until retrieved for replacement onto the skull in a later surgery, called a cranioplasty. The National Institute of Health (NIH) states that this method is a "very inexpensive option that preserves the viability of the bone flap, which can be ultimately responsible for the good cosmetic results and the very low infection rate" (https://

www.ncbi.nlm.nih.gov/pubmed/20920941). In plain terms, this is the best method for preserving the live tissues of the bone flap, and it minimizes any complications from potential infections that might occur during cranioplasty, as well as preserving the best cosmetic "fit" when the bone flap is replaced.

However, just like any other surgical procedure, placing the bone flap inside the patient in this manner does inevitably carry the risk of infection, however slight. Here again, such an infection would most likely be something of a minor nuisance to a patient whose overall physiological state was otherwise operating normally. But as he worked quickly but methodically in the operating room, Dr. Altschuler feared that Preston's immune system was so badly damaged and so severely compromised that even the slightest potential of introducing any new infections simply posed too great a risk; that even the most trivial of bacteriological infections could kill him because his immune system would be utterly powerless and unable to fight it off. So he opted not to place the large bone flap inside Preston's abdomen.

And with that, convinced that he had done everything he could to save Preston's life, but soberly uncertain about my son's immediate chances for survival, Dr. Altschuler snapped off his latex surgical gloves, scrubbed up, and went home.

As a brief side note, in these days of often outrageously overpaid athletic professional sports "superheroes" whose only contribution to society—let's state the truth with utterly unabashed honesty here—is playing a well-executed game for the sole purpose of entertainment, I have come to believe that our society is perhaps not well versed in what a real, honest-to-goodness superhero truly is, or what one actually looks like. In our family's case, Drs. Artschuler and Bursick, whose "heroic" costumes consist simply of their drab yet enormously reassuring mint-green scrubs, were the ones who utilized their superhuman medical knowledge and surgical skills to perform a miracle to save my son's life. Doctors are among our true heroes; the men and women who, through eyes strained and bloodshot have spent countless hours of sleepless nights in intensive, sometimes tedious study, or who have restlessly paced the cold dark, eerie hallways of hospital wards and medical clinics feverishly mulling over complex treatment option's or brainstorming what more can be done for their most critical patients.

Many people will not understand this until misfortune or personal catastrophe forces them to reach out for a physician's expertise during their own dark and desperate times, as we were obliged to do. These superheroes I am speaking of live among us, they look like us and maybe even attend the same athletic games we do, watching their own children playing sports that are not without risk of physical injury, but they are so much more than most of us. They are the superheroes whose sole desire and purpose of saving lives is something that we as a society desperately need and so often rely on. They keep watch over us, teach us and of course, more often than we seem to realize, they are the ones that when tragedy strikes, saves us.

Box 5.1. Preston's Mission

> *"To fear death is nothing other than to think oneself wise when one is not. For it is to think one knows what one does not know. No one knows whether death may not even turn out to be the greatest blessings of human beings. And yet people fear it as if they knew for certain it is the greatest evil."*

—Socrates

Death of course rarely reveals its exact place and time to most people and to Preston this realm of darkness came for my son after suffering three bouts of respiratory failure and cardiac arrest. In one moment, there was so much noise, so much light, so much pain, thrust upon him on that fateful day on November 5th in 2005, then sudden stillness and total darkness. It was about a year after his near-death injury where out of nowhere and much to my surprise Preston began to tell me about his experience in another realm of existence. What I am about to tell you, while hesitant to some degree, took quite some time to write as each word had to be spelled out by using his communication board.

There was no more pain, there was an absence of fear as he felt himself being pulled toward a brilliant unblinding bright white light that slowly enveloped the empty stark darkness. This welcoming beautiful ray of light began drawing him in by its force of unconditional and absolute love. Imagine it like a magnetic metal heart broken in two, where one side of the metal heart being pulled like a magnet towards the other half of the metal heart where they would connect perfectly and make whole. In the distance at the end of this bright light there is a figure, wearing a long white gown and shoulder length brown hair, faceless features however a masculine presence is sensed walking toward him. Preston drops to a knee as feeling unworthy wrapping his arms around this overwhelming presence. This figure bends over and wraps his loving arms around him like the wings of an angel softly caressing him in a tender embrace. There arises a feeling of complete overwhelming joy, love and happiness, a feeling of emancipation, of coming home. Being lifted by this presence, they begin to walk side by side, on a field of luminous long blades of grass blowing beautifully and gently in wind. They come upon two soaring resplendent trees one appearing somewhat larger than the other. Whilst standing between these two towering trees the larger of the two trees begins casting its leaves into the whispering wind ascending them upwards. While at this same moment the other but smaller tree begins to blossom presenting unparalleled color, beauty and grace while possessing an incredible powerful stance of glorious love-filled grandeur. Then suddenly, just like that it's over and the darkness returns. I am left speechless, yet in awe and craving for more.

That's it! "Preston!" I exclaimed "Do you remember anything of a conversation?" He sadly shakes his no. I sat back in my chair fully deflated. I cannot say that I was not disappointed, I was! I wish that I could understand why he does not remember what was said and left only to remember the experience. I can only surmise it's like when you awake from a dream and do not remember it but know you had one. Someone once told me that your spiritual guide chooses whether you should remember or not. So now, I am at loss as to the significance of him positioned between these two trees. What did this mean? I can only speculate that since trees seem to be the representation of life that one tree symbolized Preston life as it was, and the other one as it would be if he was to return to his body. It is absolutely amazing to me that with all the vast damage Preston's brain sustained that he could even remember this experience at all! It has affected his life so much that he insisted without debate to be included in this book. There is so much that we do not understand about our human experience, but I have come to believe through Preston's encounter that our earthly existence, our physical body, is completely separate from our consciousness, our soul. Thus, began my own personal journey towards fulfilling a loving and unconditional relationship with God and no fear of death. Regardless, there must be some importance for Preston's beating an otherwise looming death and subsequent return to this world that only his subconscious must know, maybe it was so that I could write this book!

CHAPTER 6

A WING AND A PRAYER

"There is no greater pain than to be helpless
in the face of a loved one's suffering."

—Author Unknown

There's something quite peculiar about air travel that makes the tight space inside the fuselage of an airplane an oddly good place for meditative contemplation. Once in flight, there's that ever-present and familiar rattling hum of the turbojet engines that continually reverberates through your body. And truthfully, as background noise goes, it's often quite loud inside the cabin; a fact that might be a little unnerving to the uninitiated, yet actually comforting in its reliability, if you are able to think of that monotonous droning sound as a persistent indicator that those engines are working just fine, winging you safely and securely to your desired destination. Captive in your seat, however, that metallic, mechanical hum makes conversation somewhat difficult, yet not unlike the long, continuous "Om" of the transcendental meditative state, the sound can have the effect of enveloping you in contemplative introspection and peaceful mindfulness. After all, there's not much else for you to do, especially when you didn't have time to grab a sensational novel off the shelf at the airport bookstore before you boarded without a nanosecond to spare. Like I would have been psychologically able to read in the state of anxiety that I was in anyway.

I tried to glance as unobtrusively as I could at Perry sitting next to me, not wanting to upset him or make him feel any more uncomfortable than he already was. Perry, for his part, was sitting there so profoundly quiet, so young and impressionable and now, seeming to be so emotionless and numb to this unfolding, heartbreaking situation. He appeared to be staring straight ahead at the seatback in front of him, as if in a trance, and it worried me.

What is he thinking? I wondered. *He's way too quiet.*

I wanted to talk to him. I wanted to tell him that I was here for him, that he can rest his head on my shoulder as I comfort him. But I couldn't seem to speak the words; I couldn't even seem to move at all, paralyzed by a mix of dread and uncertainty. *What kind of mother am I?* I thought. Parents' Day at Marlboro High was supposed to be special for Perry and his fellow senior teammates. I thought about how, hours earlier, proudly positioned on either side of our son, Ted and I were accorded the privilege of escorting Perry onto the field—our youngest son clad in his navy blue and gold Mustang uniform proudly displaying his number 21 and with the name "PLEVRETES" in all capital letters splashed majestically across the back of his jersey—as we and the whole Marlboro High School community collectively celebrated his final season as a high school football player. It was supposed to be *his* day, and yet here we were completely focused on his big brother Preston, the celebration of Perry's day to shine having been abruptly aborted. Thus, ripped away from perhaps the most momentous event of his young life up to that time, Perry seemed to become at times irritated and yet hauntingly quiet. At other moments he seemed confused and hurt. Things had clearly not gone as he expected they would on his big day.

Perhaps I should have realized it sooner, and more concretely, but I suspect that it was amid the disconnected, humming silence of that plane ride, tormented by the uneasy desolation and powerlessness we all must have felt, that we began to lose Perry as an integral member of our family, like a satellite that suddenly, inexplicably, begins to veer out of orbit and spiral away into the distant cosmos.

I lay my head back, my tears saturating every eyelash and bonding them together like some sort of gluey substance, making any effort to open them seem challenging enough and not worth the effort. Lulled by that continuously whirring background noise of the plane's engines, my eyes closed, my mind gradually slips back and recalls the time I heard the sound of unidentified items crashing to the floor just above my head, upstairs in one of the boys' rooms, followed almost immediately by the thunderous racing steps of my two young boys pounding down the stairs as if the world was coming to an end. Perry's nervous panting revealing a panic in progress and his running to me for some kind of salvation and protection as he is being hotly pursued by an enraged Preston. Desperately trying to calm the situation down and find out what has happened I demand that the boys sit down on the couch, one on each polar end. This was always done whenever a family meeting was in order.

As I sat there on the plane, I honestly could not recall what this particular battle was about, and of course there were many such incidents over the years, as brothers will always tend to fight. However, what I do remember with crystal clarity, and will never forget about this particular incident, was the poignant statement that Preston said to me shortly after the incident. Like many mothers I have always had that motherly, instinctively protective reaction to shield the younger and physically much smaller Perry against the formidable physical specimen that was his older sibling in those days. So, when the discussion was over and Perry had wandered back upstairs, I grabbed Preston's arm firmly and said to him with sincere concern, "Preston, one day your brother is going to hate you if you keep fighting with him." And without any hesitation and displaying a certain childlike and quizzical expression of "huh?", as if my fears made absolutely no sense to him, and as well, using all of his reassuring boyishly loveable yet bedeviling charm, Preston simply smiled and replied, "Oh Ma, Perry is my best friend and always will be, you worry too much."

* * * * *

Because we touched down at Pittsburgh International Airport a half hour ahead of schedule, the car that LaSalle's Coach had arranged for us hadn't arrived yet. I was far too anxious to wait for it, so we immediately grabbed a cab to Mercy Hospital. My heart was beating faster and faster in anticipation—and trepidation—of at last being with Preston but not knowing what his condition was, and of course fearing the worst. All we knew at that point was that he was out of surgery, as LaSalle's Coach had informed us by phone at the ticket counter back in Philadelphia—by now that felt like it was eons ago. So too, the drive from the airport to the hospital seemed like an eternity. Suddenly, I got scared; almost panicky. My hands were clammy, my eyes swollen from hours of crying, and my mind filled with the excruciating fear of what we were going to see when we got there. It's so painfully ironic; all this time I could not wait to get to Preston's side, had profusely thanked God for every curious, fortunate yet unexplainable happenstance that had miraculously occurred to speed our journey. Now that the moment was near, I was so terribly frightened of what we would face ahead. As we rushed through the hospital doors into the emergency room lobby we were told that we had to wait for a social worker who would take us to him.

My mind reeled with foreboding anguish. *Why do we need to see a social worker?* I wondered. I suddenly and fearfully thought, *Oh my God, this is the end; Preston is dead!* My inner soul was shaking, and I had to take deep breaths to calm myself down while we waited for this social worker. The second she arrived, I blurted out, "How is my son?!" And in that infernally damnable way that subordinate authority types solely possessing critical information so often seem to do, she would not answer immediately, instead instructing us to follow her to a nearby private room. It was the longest short walk of my life.

"Please," I begged the second she shut the door, "How is our son?"

She turned to us and explained that Preston was in critical condition and that his vital signs were unstable and not within normal limits. She confirmed what we already knew that he was out of surgery and in the intensive care trauma unit, but then she added ominously that her sole purpose was to prepare us for what we were about to see. She explained that Preston had a very serious brain injury and was in a coma (also information we already very painfully knew), and she cautioned us not to be surprised or frightened with all machines and wires and tubes that were attached to him that were keeping him alive.

Keeping him alive!

Those three terrifying words echoed over and over again in my depleted and exhausted mind. She may have continued telling us more, but as the implications of those portentous words amplified and reverberated through my psyche, and I heard nothing else she uttered after that.

The stillness of the place was eerie, the wrenching, fearful anticipation palpable among the three of us, as the social worker soberly escorted us to the elevator. The doors kissed shut sealing us in that familiar silent vacuum as we rode up to the ICU Trauma unit. I peered through the tiny slits that were all that was left of my swollen eyes, up towards the illuminated floor numbers just above the doors as the elevator slowly made its journey upward. We were then taken to an area adjacent to Preston's room for special preparations. Due to his compromised immune system, not to mention the craniotomy, we were obliged to don protective sterile gowns and masks before we could enter. Nevertheless, standing in front of the sink washing my hands, there was a rather large picture window that looked directly into his room. And it was through that glass, into a room as dimly lighted as a funeral parlor, that I abruptly and quite unexpectedly caught my first glimpse of my beautiful boy like I'd never had to witness before. It was like being surprisingly slapped in the face by a splash of cold water. I suddenly struggled to catch my breath, propping my hands tightly on either side of the sink to quietly compose myself.

Immediately sensing my distress, the social worker gently but firmly put a hand on my shoulder and asked if I was all right. I responded with a slight nod, the only gesture I could muster; I could not speak a word. "There can be no excessive stimulation, so speak softly and only one at a time," she told us in a rather sternly authoritative voice as we entered the room.

The only way to describe this sterile chamber is that it presents as surrealistically dark all around the outer perimeter, except for a few colored, pin-prick lights on the monitoring machines, glowing amid the blackness like distant, isolated stars. A small, almost insignificant light glares down obnoxiously at the head of the hospital bed where my beautiful Preston lay in a coma, like the spotlight of a tragic play. Or perhaps, I tried to imagine, like some kind of spiritual light watching over and comforting him. The room feels very cool, exuding a mood that is profoundly somber, even funereal. The pulsating lights and sound of the machines *keeping my son alive* seem to be beating in sync to the rhythm of my own heart. From the mechanical, discordant symphony of the resonating popping and hissing sounds generated by the movement of air through the respirator that is keeping my boy breathing, to the maddening flat tone beeping shrill of the hospital monitor next to his bed displaying the visible images of his heartbeat, blood pressure, and most crucially, his brain activity, it is all psychologically and emotionally devastating to have to gaze upon a loved one in such a state, especially one's own child.

The social worker needn't have been so concerned about overstimulation, because as I moved toward his bedside, I was barely able even so much as to utter any recognizable words or sound. I felt like a bug trapped in amber. My anxiety reached such a torturous pinnacle that my legs began to quiver, and it was all I could do to prevent myself from falling flat onto the polished vinyl floor. I reached for his arm and bent over softly toward his beautiful, strangely peaceful, yet ominously expressionless face full of wires and tubes, and I quietly whisper, "Preston we are all here with you and we love you. You are in the hospital and you are going to be alright. Can you hear me? Squeeze my hand and show me a sign you can hear me." But he lay there unresponsive, as if trapped in the deepest, most cognitively distant sleep of his life, and I feel completely numb and desperately powerless… and overwhelmingly defeated.

It was at that moment that all my frenzied emotions had reached its peak and I finally crashed; there was nothing left of me, lacking all sensations except the sorrowful expression of my grief rising from the deepest pit of my soul. "His body does not look real to me," I whispered to Ted. His hands were cold to the touch, his skin appearing so taught and smooth, tinted a cruel blanch white. I could not sense his presence or his energy, the inner essence of his being the way only a mother can; just a cold stillness, as if all that remained was the vacant shell of his physical body. He showed no reaction to stimuli of any kind; it was as if the very current of his vital life force has been turned off like a light switch on the wall.

What can I do? My mother's instinct is to move heaven and earth to make everything all well, but of course this is not within my power to do. I feel so helpless, so powerless even to simply comfort him in the unsounded and unfathomable depths of his present unconsciousness, much less make it all better. So many thought-provoking questions are running through my psyche, yet the loudest and the most imponderable one is: *Why?*

Why did this happen?

He was only 19 years old with so much of life ahead, yet now all of his hopes, dreams, aspirations, relationships—his very independence as a human being with so much of himself to give—all of this vanishes in a cataclysmic and terrible instant. Overcome with grief, I fell heavily into to a chair to pray. "Dear God in heaven, if he is there with you now, please give him back to us, I beseech you; we love him so much."

At the end of Preston's bed stands Perry, silent yet quite stoic balancing between his inner thoughts of this reality and his own surreal imagination as he gazes upon Preston. Without warning he unexpectedly whips out his phone and takes a couple of pictures of Preston immortalizing the moment. At first, I felt that taking these pictures seemed disrespectful and crass, however in a peculiar sort of way I understood why it was necessary for him to take them. Preston, who he perceived was so resilient and invincible, was going to wake up from this slumber in good health and they would both would have a good laugh later while viewing the pictures.

"We suffer more often in imagination than in realty"

– L.A. Seneca

* * * * *

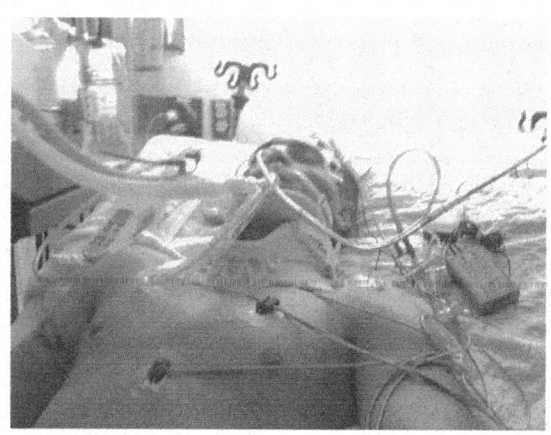

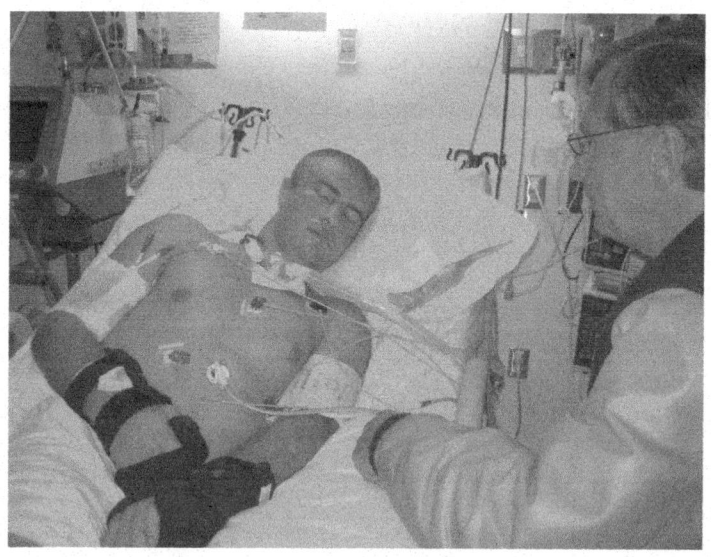

Suddenly all hell seems to break loose as the regular metronomic pulsing beep of the heart monitor blasts into a loud warning scream, lights flashing madly. Preston's eyes are shockingly wide open, his jaw is tightly clenched, his arms go rigid, extending straight down at his side rotating towards the back of his fists to face upward. For many terrible seconds he looks horribly like a man who has just been electrocuted but as though the voltage hadn't yet finished its deadly work. The trauma team of nurses and doctors came rushing in, wordlessly ushering us out of the way as they work feverishly to stabilize Preston. As they work they explain curtly that this type of phenomenon occurs when a stimulus such as pain causes the working set of muscles to contract, often powerfully. Preston is going into decerebrate posturing!

I am terrified to witness this episode, both my hands drawn to mask my mouth to hold back my horrified screams, yet wretchedly frustrated that I as a mother could do nothing to fix what was occurring before my eyes. It was just like Preston on that Duquesne football field, his mind exploding in pain and crying out just one more time the best he could, trying urgently to tell us, "Help me, I'm hurting! I want to live!" *Dear God, what is happening?* I wondered, struggling to not panic.

They proceed to tie his arms to the bed rails, and I ask what was happening and why do they need to tie him down? A foolish question, in a way, and of course they explain hastily that they want to prevent Preston from hurting himself. Then someone said, "This is the body's response to a severe brain stem injury." With that I began repeating a new and frightening script in my mind; *brain stem injury, brain stem injury…. what brain stem injury are they talking about?* No one had said anything to us about a brain stem injury, and so now I start to worry about this as well; what kind of negative impact will this latest cruel complication have on my son? I know enough about the brain stem to know that it regulates the most basic, primordial internal systems and motor functions of the body. Will this added injury affect his ability to breathe, maintain normal blood pressure and body temperature so that he can continue to live a normal life? Will it prevent his immune system from protecting his body from other kinds of infections or diseases? Or was Preston's short time here on earth expiring right in front of us? Was this the catastrophically unimaginable end of the master blueprint of life that Preston had all planned out for himself? The end of his destiny?

Finally, and mercifully, the trauma medical team is able to stabilize Preston and his muscles start to relax, his eyes closing as he appears to descend back into his suspended, unknowable state of being, of a kind of suspended animation. And it was then that I realized we would need a lot more answers about all of the factors affecting my son's medical condition—and his very hold on life itself. Some of those answers would soon be forthcoming, yet others would take many years (and still remain unresolved), and those complex and interconnected factors would be staggering in both number and degree of severity.

* * * * *

No one had noticed that the sun had set, and that the night had quietly cantered in with all its absolute blackness. It was now late in the evening nearing midnight and after witnessing this frightening episode, we were all but left to our little moments of quiet sanity when a nurse came into the room and informed us that Dr. Altschuler, the neurosurgeon who had operated on Preston, would like to speak with us regarding his ordeal, the surgery that had been performed, and his current prognosis. The doctor was no longer on the premises at the hospital but would speak with us via speaker phone in a private room.

I will never forget the first bitter, petrifying words Dr. Altschuler said in no uncertain terms when he opened the conversation: "Preston is in critical condition and I'm not sure if he will make it through the night." Brutally candid, perhaps, but the truth was that we wanted only the truth no matter how dire Preston's situation was. As you would expect, we wanted to know everything that happened from the moment the neurosurgeon first saw Preston to the point where came out of surgery, which Dr. Altschuler, very patiently, and with a doctor's precision, went on to describe in detail.

Have you ever been in that strange, surreal state of mind where you know, sort of semi-consciously, that you are in a given place, yet you feel as though you are not there at all, and that you are viewing the proceedings around you as if you are an ethereal apparition, both invisible to and beyond the hearing of everyone else? That's how I felt in that room. I think my mind was shot—cognitively, psychologically, emotionally, and more. There were a million questions pinwheeling through my mind, but after everything that we had been through that day, the frenzied juggernaut to Pittsburgh by car and plane, I was no longer able rationally to define and articulate them.

Quite fortunately, for starters at least, it was La Salle's football coach who first asked one of them—and it was a very potently critical one. (LaSalle's coach asking the question may be the only reason I remember that he was one of the people who had joined Ted, Perry, and me in the room during our conference with Dr. Altschuler; there may have been one or two La Salle athletic department employees there, but I just don't remember anymore.)

In any case, the Coach asked, "Was this a blood clot that had been there awhile?" Dr. Altschuler replied, "This did cross our minds because he had such a severe amount of bleeding and we had such a terrible time trying to control it. I wondered if there had been some underlying vascular malformation that contributed to the extreme severity of the subdural hematoma."

In fact, the neurosurgeon's suspicion that Preston's massive bleeding may have involved a previous injury was so strong that he consequently ordered another test to be performed, called a CT Angiogram. And while this test showed no clear-cut evidence of a pre-existing injury, Dr. Altschuler pointed out that while the CT would have very reliably indicated a large vascular malformation, if one existed, his concern was over the possibility that the CT might fail to pick up a relatively small one that would have been just as dangerous to Preston. Not only that, but the CT Angiogram came back with a strong recommendation for a more sophisticated version of the test, in which a catheter is inserted into one of the large arteries of the leg and the sensor is carefully threaded up into the patient's brain to obtain a more sensitive and accurate reading.

However, Dr. Altschuler indicated that Preston was so severely neurologically (and physically) injured that, whatever the more formal CT Angiogram would have found, "we wouldn't have altered our treatment in the OR. We were more interested in his recovery… than investigating a further etiology for his bleed." I realized that this language was calm, cool, and very professionally understated doctor-speak for, "We were solely focused on saving Preston's life."

Oh My God, to the best of my layman's understanding, was he essentially saying that Preston's brain exploded? This was devastating news! Now even more utterly confused, I thought, *what do we do now?* I could not speak. Ted and the coach were asking all kinds of questions, but I could not utter a single word. Why could I not speak? I could not muster the ability to formulate any rational questions; my mind was depleted and useless. All I kept thinking was: *Why did this happen? WHY??* I did not want to hear anything more, I wanted to escape this room and be with my son, my Preston.

* * * * *

After that bleak and distressing consultation with Dr. Altschuler, we all went back to Preston's room, where it seemed there was absolutely nothing further I could say or even think; and certainly nothing I could do to make any of this any better. Preston's prognosis landed like a bomb, frightening and disorienting all of us in a way that few other kinds of calamities in one's life, or in one's family, can do.

Before me in this cold, darkened, and palpably isolated room, my dearest son lay in a coma, caused by a life-threatening injury sustained in this All-American game of football. My distraught mind bitterly descended into a complicated mix of disheartening confusion and a resigned yet incredulous understanding, that a mere game, and something that Preston so loved passionately, could be so dreadfully deadly. It defied all beliefs... football! Football had always been a part of our family life. I thought about how my husband Ted in his early years played semi-pro ball, and how both our boys played from their earliest years in Pop Warner, up through high school, and now for Preston, in college. I suppose vaguely and somehow distantly, throughout these years there had always been an unspoken understanding that football, simply due to the nature of this high impact, contact sport, might inflict upon even the best of players a broken arm or a busted knee, but I had never imagined a broken life.

Or even a lost one: So precariously uncertain was Preston's very hold on life, that we summoned a priest to administer holy last rites, just in case he should pass from this earth sometime before the night was over.

* * * * *

I was informed by the hospital staff that I needed to retrieve Preston's uniform and give it back to La Salle University. It was a dark and gloominess place located at a lower level of the hospital with the feeling of a garage. When I got up to the window I said to the elderly gentleman who was listening to some oldies playing on the small radio he had on his desk; "I am here to pick up the personal items for my son Preston Plevretes." The man looked up at me and said sympathetically; "Oh…. the football player. How is he doing?" "He's doing the best he can" I replied not really wanting to talk about it. He then handed over to me these soiled, rigid, remarkable pieces of clothing now laying across my arms, reflecting its memory of a young man's vitality, energy and spirit. As I walk over to the elevator I gazed down at them as some of the dried dirt and bits of grass flake off onto the floor, I noticed that the shirt has been cut in half, straight up the middle from the waist to the neck, probably from the ER staff or perhaps on the field by the EMT's, I don't know. I succumb to the temptation and slowly raised his shirt to my face still lingering with the smell of his sacrificial sweat, mingled with the scent of the freshly cut grass surrendering Preston's fate as another fallen warrior on the field of conquest and I fall to my knees. I have already cried too many tears, but these damn emotions of grief are raging inside from the very depths of my soul and won't let go, rapidly spinning like a tornado, a storm of sorrows that dare to cry out "Oh God, why did this happen!" NO, I don't want to give them back his uniform, it holds the very last essence of my son's past 19 years. Augh……..I cry out so raw from the pit of my soul, the pain, it hurts. What am I thinking, YES, give it back to them, I hate them, I don't want to see them, I don't want to be reminded of that thief that stole my son's dreams, and pilfered his destiny. I am all the sudden overcome by an intense feeling of guilt, why did I not truly understand how risky football really was or was I just blind.

It was getting late, and the Mercy hospital administration staff was kind enough to give us a "relatives' room," on one of the upper floors, where we could stay for the night. I told them that I wanted to stay with Preston, but they told me that would not be possible; nor was it advisable, they said, because Preston needed to get rest and so did we. This time, I have to say the hospital officials or staff were right, and they assured me that they would call us immediately if anything were to happen overnight. I obliged myself to be satisfied with that, because I knew that Perry, for one, desperately needed to get some rest.

Nevertheless reluctant, Ted, Perry and I were escorted to a small room a couple floors up from the Trauma Unit where there were two twin beds and a small bathroom. Perry was extremely tired and went immediately to sleep, while Ted and I lay on top of the covers on the other bed, helplessly wide awake, yet neither acknowledging to the other that we were waiting in anguished dread for the phone to ring. It had been a very traumatic day for all of us. I remember looking over at Perry and wondering how he was able to sleep so soundly. Was that simply the boundless resiliency of youth, or was he just utterly too exhausted to even be capable of staying awake? After all, it was almost incomprehensible, in the midst of the darkness of the night, to remember that he had played a full game of football back in New Jersey earlier that same day. Myself unable to sleep, I got up and started pacing the floor, praying and pleading with God to wake my son Preston from this unrelenting nightmare.

Then suddenly, the phone rang. The sound of it seemed louder than any ringing phone I'd ever heard in my entire life.

Ted sat up from the bed; he was barely in reach of the phone, yet he remained there rigidly upright, as if abruptly frozen in place and unable to move any further. I rushed over to the nightstand where the phone was located, but we both paused for a moment, just staring at the phone, both too terrified to pick it up, fearful of what news will emanate from the other end. "I can't answer it," I said finally, as I slowly sat down on the bed next to him. And in a manner that might have suggested that this grave duty was the husband's job in this situation, Ted picked up the phone and with a soft, restrained... anxious voice, he said, "Hello?" My heart was pounding with the fear that the news at that moment would be that our boy was dead; I was already on the verge of weeping again. But then Ted looked at me and exhaled a heavy sigh of relief releasing all the tension from his upper body and he relaxed. He then said to the Trauma Nurse at the other end of the call, "Oh okay, sure. Please put her through." I looked at Ted with confusion, but he held up a flat hand and shook his head reassuringly, as if to say everything was okay.

"Hi Jillian," he said, and I clutched my shirt with both hands, in the area nearest my heart, as I released my own sigh of relief. Jillian, Preston's girlfriend from high school and panic-stricken after having heard about Preston's injury on the field, was calling desperately in the middle of the night, trying to find out if he was alright. She was distraught, and that's putting it mildly, because all I could hear through the earpiece was her wailing uncontrollably on the other end of the call. Ted tried to calm her down, telling her honestly that Preston was alive but critical, and that he would call her tomorrow with any updated news.

It was neither the potentially terrifying call telling us that Preston's fight was over, and that he was gone, nor the one, admittedly based solely in absurd fantasy unfortunately, in which the caller would have said that he "miraculously" woke up and started talking. But it did remind me that there were a lot of good people back home who were thinking and pulling and praying for Preston, who cared about a young man who was beloved by many in our community. After Ted hung up, nothing was said. My husband lay back down on the bed, while I got up and returned to pacing the floor.

*   *   *   *   *

Dr. Altschuler would later say that Preston's was the worst athletic brain injury he had ever seen, likening it to something one might expect to see as a result of a high-speed head-on automobile collision. "I think the reason [Preston's] still alive," Altschuler said shortly after the operation, "is because he's in such top physical shape. He has such a strong heart." I personally believe it was the vibrant and determined life force of a young man, an Aries no less, a determined and resilient young man who was adamantly not ready to die.

PART II

The Forever Injury

CHAPTER 7

SECOND IMPACT SYNDROME

*"Football is a game of chance.
A chance unscathed, a chance scarred or a chance to die."*

– Tammy Plevretes

It is crucial to explain what really happened to Preston. The grievous and life-altering injury that my son sustained on the football field on November 5th, 2005 is what is known as Second Impact Syndrome (SIS). It is a rare but singularly catastrophic event that occurs only to athletes or other individuals under the age of 23 whose brains have not yet fully formed. As the name suggests, the syndrome occurs when an athlete who sustains a head injury—often a concussion or worse injury, such as a cerebral contusion—sustains a second head injury before symptoms associated with the first have fully cleared or healed.

The heightened potential of catastrophic brain injury resulting from second impact syndrome was first described by Richard Schneider in 1973 in his study of two young athletes, each of whom experienced initial concussive incidents, went back out onto the playing field, and subsequently died after each sustained relatively minor second head injuries. The term itself, *second impact syndrome*, was coined by doctors Richard Saunders and Robert Harbaugh in their 1984 article published in the *Journal of the American Medical Association*. Like Schneider, Saunders and Harbaugh described the case of a 19-year-old college football player—coincidently the same age as Preston at the time of his injury—who suffered an initial head injury with brief loss of consciousness. And much like Preston—shudderingly so in my mind—the 19-year-old in their report returned to play almost immediately despite repeated complaints of persistent headaches. Four days later, that athlete collapsed on the practice field, became unresponsive, and died; a fate that would no doubt have befallen my son, as we have seen, had the circumstances of proximity to the hospital been different, and certainly without the heroic work of Drs. Altschuler and Bursick. In fact, most victims of SIS do not survive.

Yet, one of the surprising aspects of SIS is that the second event or hit may be relatively minor in nature, perhaps only involving a blow to the chest that jerks or jars the athlete's head and only indirectly imparts accelerative forces to the brain, in essence banging an already bruised brain around inside the skull. In a report evaluating Preston's injury, Dr. Robert Cantu, Chief of Neurosurgery and Director of Sports Medicine at Emerson Hospital in Boston and Medical Director for the National Center for Catastrophic Sports Injury Research (NCCSIR), is one of the country's leading experts on sports related cervical spine and head injuries, observed that, "Affected athletes may appear stunned but usually do not lose consciousness and often complete the play," adding that, "They usually remain on their feet for 15 seconds to one minute or so, but seem dazed, like someone suffering with a Grade 1 concussion without the loss of consciousness."

However, the rapidly unfolding and virtually uncontrollable course of SIS from this point is what makes the syndrome so deadly, according to Dr. Cantu. He states: "What happens in the next 15 seconds to several minutes sets this syndrome [SIS] apart from a concussion. Usually within… minutes of the second impact, the athlete—conscious yet stunned—quite precipitously collapses to the ground, semi-comatose with rapidly dilating pupils, loss of eye movement, and evidence of respiratory failure."

The game against Duquesne was being broadcast on local television, so there exists for eternity actual film footage of the fateful hit that nearly ended Preston's life. As described earlier, the film appears to confirm that the hit, as vicious as it was, was nevertheless perfectly legal under the rules of the game. As such, for example, the film also appears to confirm that there was no helmet-to-helmet contact, which of course would have been illegal—and subject to a 15-yard penalty, for what that's worth. Dr. Micky Collins is an internationally recognized expert in sports-related concussion, and the Director of the Sports Medicine Concussion Program at the University of Pittsburgh Medical Center (UPMC), the first and largest research and clinical program focused on the diagnosis, evaluation and management of sports-related mild traumatic brain injury in athletes of all levels. In reviewing Preston's medical records including the film footage of the on-field collision, Dr. Collins asserted in an ESPN interview, "I don't believe the second event would have ended up resulting in a catastrophic outcome if it weren't for the first concussion occurring." Indeed, many experts who have reviewed Preston's case believe that were it not for the first concussion, Preston would have gotten right up off the ground and resumed play over the course of the waning minutes of the game against Duquesne that day. What I believe—and know of a certainty—is that if my son had been properly diagnosed and treated after the first concussion, if he had been properly examined and tested by a qualified physician, and even if the then-existing protocols governing the clearance of concussive athletes to resume play had been followed (weak as they were in the college game in 2005), Preston would very likely be perfectly fine today. Even if that meant sitting out the remainder of the whole damn season at La Salle.

In his report, Dr. Cantu touched briefly on what is presently known about the pathophysiology of SIS, which is believed to involve the loss of autoregulation of the brain's blood supply. Medical researchers Wetjen, Pichelmann, and Atkinson (2010) describe cerebral autoregulation as "the 'tone' the arterial tree assumes to... keep cerebral blood flow constant under normal conditions" (p. 553). Cantu notes that "The loss of autoregulation leads to vascular engorgement within the cranium, which, in turn, markedly increases intracranial pressure and leads to herniation either of the medial surface of the temporal lobes [that is, the lobes of the cerebrum] or the lobes below the tentorium of the cerebellar tonsils [that is, the cerebellum] through the foramen magnum" [i.e., the hole in the base of the skull through which the spinal cord passes]. That's more or less a long medical way of saying, as I lamented earlier, that Preston's brain essentially "exploded"—not by literally being "blown apart" as happens for example when dynamite or some other explosive is detonated to bring down a building, but in the sense that his brain underwent massive, almost instantaneous and uncontrollable swelling that essentially ballooned within his skull and within the space of just those several minutes immediately after the on-field impact.

In summing up his findings, Dr. Cantu wrote, "Preston did not fully recover from his October 4th concussion and was playing while symptomatic with headaches when he received his catastrophic injury…. His deterioration on the field was precipitous and consistent with second impact syndrome, as was the degree of massive brain swelling that [immediately] occurred." Cantu went so far as to suggest that the massive hematoma or blood clot that Drs. Altschuler and Bursick worked feverishly to remove upon first opening Preston's skull was far less of a concern than the rapidly progressed brain swelling itself. He wrote, "it is reasonably certain that had Preston not sustained second impact syndrome with rapid development of malignant edema, the subdural hematoma [blood clot] that Preston had would have been excisable without significant" long-term consequences. And in concluding his report, Cantu stated, "Thus, while the acute subdural hematoma required surgical excision, it was the malignant brain swelling the neurosurgeon encountered that had caused brain herniation and caused Preston's brain infarction and resultant devastating brain injury."

Yet tragically, even the "devastating brain injury" that occurred as a result of SIS would in many ways pale in comparison to the severe and further life-threatening medical complications that Preston would have to face going forward, as we will shortly see. For now, however, just the gargantuan effort that it would take to get Preston home to New Jersey would prove to be a frightening, nerve-wracking ordeal during which I unrelentingly feared for his safety and welfare—feared the distinct possibility of his sustaining yet another grievous injury during what would inevitably be an arduous transport—every minute of every hour it took to get my son home and into the first of several rehabilitation facilities.

* * * * *

You send your kids off to school and never in your worst nightmare do you ever even remotely imagine the possibility that you might either bring them home in a body bag, or in our case, strapped to a gurney inside a small, medically equipped, private charter jet in the somber grip of a devastating coma.

Even as Preston lay, comatose, in critical condition in Mercy Hospital's ICU, believe it or not there were forces at work that would put his life in danger once again. I am talking of course about our health insurer at the time, which coldly informed us after only one week in the hospital due to his catastrophic injury, that they no longer wanted to pay for Preston's hospital care services, and they summarily directed us to move him to a less expensive rehabilitation facility closer to our home. Of course, money was the operative decision-driving factor for our insurance company.

This was simply preposterous, I thought, reasoning that with his craniotomized head in its highly vulnerable present condition, he could not be moved safely. In fact, the order was downright reckless if not morally depraved in my view. Preston had no skull covering nearly half of the top of his head; there was literally only a thin layer of skin covering his exposed brain that offered little or no protection against any objects that might be accidently encountered in transit. Surely, any rough movement or, God forbid, even a minor bump to the affected area might cause more serious brain damage than he had already endured. Worse, any excessive jarring of his head or body might very conceivably induce another stroke I flat-out said this to the doctors. Preston's condition remained far too critical, and he should not be moved, I insisted, determined to hold my ground.

And while all of the doctors resolutely agreed with my assessment, they also pointed out the grim reality that the insurance company was not going to continue to pay for ICU services that were running at the prodigious rate of $13,000 a day (so we were told). We certainly did not have the personal resources needed to pay such costs. This why you have insurance! I have learned that the insurance companies are the ones who at the end seem call all of the shots. Rehabilitation hospitals were developed to meet the need for a less costly per diem than most general hospitals require in cases like Preston's, the doctors explained. Moreover, they assured us, rehab facilities are better equipped to provide a higher, more sophisticated level of care through specialized therapies such as speech, occupational and physical therapies, all things that Preston was going to eventually need—assuming he would ever come out of coma. So, we had to find a rehab facility immediately.

I did a lot of research to try to find the best rehab hospital for Preston and found Kessler Institute for Rehabilitation in New Jersey. I had heard of Kessler as a well-regarded facility, and of course, there had been a lot of relatively positive publicity about them when actor Christopher Reeves went there after his horseback riding injury. However, Kessler has a couple of facilities, one specifically for spinal injuries like that suffered by Reeves, and another devoted to brain injuries like Preston's, the latter of which is located in the town of Chester.

The problem then became: How do we get him there—and do it safely. We categorically ruled out an over-the-road ambulance drive from Pittsburgh to Kessler that would take a grueling seven hour's over unforgiving concrete interstate highways, and which the doctors felt this was far too potentially detrimental to Preston. For my part, there was no doubt in my mind that the drive could actually kill my son.

The best alternative turned out to be Life Flight, a critical care air ambulance service specially equipped as flying intensive care units. Life Flight provides a small -pressurized aircraft that enables an urgent, fast, and safe method of transport for severely injured patients. The cost to book the jet would be about $6,000 and the flight from Pittsburgh to Newark would take about two hours. However, Ted and I did not have $6,000 in cash at our immediate disposal, and the insurance company of course was not going to cover it. Fortunately, this is where La Salle University, at least in this one instance, came up big: They offered to cover the cost of the plane flight and we were very grateful.

Friday, November 18th, the day we took Preston home to New Jersey, remains an acutely harrowing memory burned into my psyche, and a day I shall never forget. If anyone needed a sign that my son was in far too critical condition to be moved, it happened the very moment the EMT's came into his room to transfer him onto the transport gurney for the short over-the-road ambulance trip to the airport.

It remains unclear why, but suddenly Preston's eyes shot shockingly wide- open and he let out a ferocious yet horribly agonizing growl unlike anything I had ever heard before. I was mortified! Acting quickly, one of the EMTs immediately grabbed some kind of tongue depressor and plunged it into Preston's mouth so that he would not bite his own tongue off. He was convulsing again, his whole body going into spasms. Think about this: Something happened that created so much pain that he responded with this quasi-cognitive outburst despite the fact that he was still deep in a profound coma. *He should not be moved!* I thought again upon witnessing this. *He has no skull! His brain is so swollen any movement might be fatal!* But in the end, there was really nothing else we could do.

Transporting Preston on a plane carried its own dangers. The pressure, noise, aerodynamic movement, gravitational forces, potential air turbulence as well as other crucial concerns all posed significant risks and only served to heighten my already considerable, mind-bending distress on this flight of misery. In yet another of the innumerable conflicts between the administration of competent and responsible, patient-centered medical care versus cold and calculated insurance company financial expediency—conflicts that fly in the face of both common sense and basic human compassion—in Mercy hospital it had been imperative, according to the doctors and nurses, that we kept Preston free from any loud noise or distractions because, we were advised, his brain could not handle excessive sensory stimulation of any kind. We had been allowed only two people at a time in his room. Yet here, in sharp contradiction to those ominous but emphatic instructions from competent doctors, we were exposing Preston to the very sorts of intense and obnoxious sensory insults that we were specifically warned could lead to further trauma and even more pervasive brain damage!

While the flight to Newark was mercifully uneventful, we would not arrive at the Kessler facility in Chester until 11:00 o'clock that evening. That was due in large part to the driver of the ambulance, who rigidly insisted on taking us to the West Orange facility despite my imploring protestations that his orders were mistaken—a fact that could have been confirmed by a simple phone call that the driver pig-headedly refused to make.

In any case, Preston was at last brought in and settled into a private room while I signed off, first on the ambulance documents, and then the hopelessly redundant patient admissions paperwork for Kessler. After completing all of the formalities, I was escorted to Preston's room. It was nearing midnight; I was physically exhausted, and psychologically frazzled, it has been a long and frightful day. I was buoyed only by the thought that Ted and Perry would be there shortly.

However, when I got to his room, the nurse who was attending to his needs appeared visibly exasperated; deep, worrisome concern showing in her contorted face. Fearing the worst, I asked her what was wrong. The words she spoke at that moment penetrated my psyche like a knife plunged through my soul.

"This boy should not be here," she angrily stammered, her eyes narrowing with the gravity of the situation. "He is far too sick!" she said.

"I knew it!" I exclaimed. "I feel the same way, but the doctors said he was ready."

The nurse replied, "Well he absolutely is not; he has a 104-degree fever with a severe brain injury and he's in a coma, for God's sake! He should be in a hospital ICU where he can be properly monitored; he is not ready for a rehab facility."

Too stunned to move, I sank into the cold unsympathetic plastic and metal chair next to Preston's bed, her distressing words reprimanding our decision for rehab was overwhelming and laid heavily on my conscience. The weight too hard to endure, my head fell into my hands and I began to sob.

"Oh my God what have we done! What have we done!" I cried. *Why did we not fight the insurance company and the hospital harder*, was all I could think, and at that very moment, Ted walked through the door to find me sobbing.

"What's wrong" he said. I told him what the nurse had said. I felt such a stinging sense of remorseful guilt rising up within me, tightening my stomach into knots and banging in my head like a hammer. I felt physically and mentally gutted.

I looked up and noticed that Ted was alone, so I asked, "Where's Perry?"

"He was very tired," Ted replied, trying his best to be sympathetic in explaining away Perry's seemingly increasing detachment. "So I dropped him off at home, told him to get some sleep." "That was best," I quietly said. That night would prove to be a long one for me and for Ted. I would stay at the hospital with Preston while Ted would embark on yet another lonely two-hour voyage back home, barely an hour after he had first arrived at Kessler, and not long after he and Perry had spent seven monotonous hours on the road from Pittsburgh because there was only room for one passenger on the Life Flight plane, which I was elected.

Kessler was kind enough to provide me with a spare bed next to Preston's and throughout the night all I heard was the desperate moaning of other patients on the ward. A distraught woman across the hall kept yelling, "Help me, help me!" throughout the night. When I inquired about her in the morning, I was told she had Alzheimer's and did this all the time. But the most troubling and depressing visions appeared when I walked the halls, where patients, mostly ashen-faced elderly sat tragically alone in their wheelchairs lined up along the wall; just mindlessly sitting there woefully unattended. Waiting for someone to acknowledge them perhaps, to just tell them that they are loved, cared for, that they mattered. While my heart and mind filled with such profound sympathy and sorrow for these lonely patients I became deeply distressed that this woeful place may do more harm for Preston and it was simply too much for me to bear. So, I decided that very first night that I did not want my son to stay here!

Of deeper concern, however, it quickly became evident that Preston was growing weaker. The rehab doctors could not control his fever and his brain was swelling again, alarmingly so. He was slipping away from us again. It was decided that Preston should be put back in the hospital immediately, as it appeared that we were rapidly losing him. So just three days after he was removed from Mercy against my better judgement, on November 22, which happened to be Ted's 60th birthday, his son of just 19 years old was put back into ICU at Memorial Hospital in Morristown in critical condition. It was at this point in my grieving process, I believe, that I moved from feeling sad and ineffectual to being angry and determined to put a stop to this nonsense, to make sure that this would never happen again.

Preston was in ICU for a few of days to stabilize his brain swelling and address his ongoing 104-degree temperature. Once the swelling was under control he was transferred to a step-down unit. One thing I was insistent about was that a notice be placed on the wall at the head of Preston's bed reminding everyone that he had no skull on his right side of his head. This was to inform the seemingly endless stream of doctors, nurses and aides that were in and out of his room for various duties I couldn't even keep track of. Since this notice was inadvertently left in ICU I went to the nurse's desk to ask to have another notice prepared and placed on the wall behind him. I was shocked when she told me that she could not do this without a direct order from the doctor! I glared at her for moment, and said finally, "Can I have a piece of paper please, and a pen." She eyed me suspiciously as she reluctantly handed me these items, and she watched, speaking not a word, as I defiantly prepared the notice myself. I gave her back her pen and proceeded to post the notice up myself. I had reached the very limit of my tolerance for hospital bureaucratic mentality that seemed almost deliberately designed to deny or reject plain common sense and due precautionary diligence.

Once his condition stabilized, Preston was moved to a regular room as we searched for a better rehab hospital for him. I did not want to take him back to Kessler. Instead, fortunately, we found a much better choice for him at the JFK Medical Center and Neuroscience Institute in Edison, NJ. This facility was only about 30 minutes from our home, but most importantly, at the time (and perhaps still today) the Neuroscience Institute was rated as the number one hospital in New Jersey for the treatment of stroke and complex neurological disorders. It was the place we should have taken Preston to begin with, but admittedly, we were blindly captivated by Kessler's marquee name.

As that sad and tragic month of November 2005 came to an end, we received word that Preston would finally be moved to JFK on the second of December. So, on the evening of the 1st, I decided to stay overnight in the hospital with my son, since his transport was scheduled for the crack of dawn. It was important that I accompany Preston's transfer so that I could keep his head from bouncing around from the rough roads as he had no skull to protect his very fragile brain from further damage. Sitting again in that hard and distinctly uncomfortable cafeteria-style plastic chair with metal legs that grated on the tile floor, I lay my heavy head on a small area at the corner of Preston's bed and closed my eyes, I was very tired.

Preston's room was dark and quiet, just the faint and eerie light emanating from the hall through the slightly opened doorway and the now familiar beeping hum of the monitors telling me all was well. Just as I began to drift off a nurse came bursting in and said, "I'm sorry, but visiting hours are over and you can't stay here. You must leave."

Exhausted and rather irritated, I looked up at her through languid eyes and said dully, "I am staying."

Taken aback, the nurse replied in obvious consternation, "Well, what do I tell my supervisor?"

"You tell your supervisor to talk to me," I said firmly, and then gently laid my head back down on Preston's bed.

The nurse turned and left, closing the door behind her. No one bothered me again for the rest of the night.

CHAPTER 8

TEN YARDS AT A TIME ANALOGY: FOOTBALL'S DIRTY LITTLE SECRET

"In life, as in football, the principle to follow is to hit the line hard."

—President Theodore Roosevelt

I can understand this love of football. It is certainly an action-packed, complex, and exciting game. For those who play it, I can only imagine the kind of adrenaline rush that is experienced in the hard-hitting on-field combat that attends every game. Yet even for mere spectators a football match provides a certain euphoric, breathtaking natural high whether one actually attends a live game at the stadium or simply watches on television at home among a gathering of family and friends—and where in fact the dozens of camera angles and instant replays bring the hits viscerally into one's living room. I get it, and I have been to many games both on the scholastic level and at the professional level, as well as hosting many Super Bowl parties in our football loving home. For all that it offers, I have always loved the game, too.

While the issue of whether competitive sports builds character, or whether that is a convenient myth for proponents of the game, has been debated for decades, I feel that it is fair to say, at a minimum, that football may well indeed help to teach kids many of life's lessons—a fact that has more to say about why I've loved this game and bought into it as an endeavor that would be good for my kids.

Football has typically been used as a metaphor for life itself, for example using the 10 yards at a time analogy that was taught. The first ten yards are exhilarating, you are eager to learn and ready to take on the challenges; it instills social skills, values, and teamwork as you and your teammates forge your way to the next 10-yard line and confront a new set of downs. The next ten yards the hits keep coming, but you battle on because you have been infused with discipline and determination to move that ball of life forward to your next 10-yard goal. The next ten yards you may be getting tired, fumble, experience frustrations, losses, adversities may come, any sympathy for you is absent, but relentless perseverance surpasses these blocks and tackles, only strengthening your resolve to reach that goal line and succeed. When failure inevitably arrives, you adjust and change your tactics and keep moving forward, just ten yards more and you have proven through sacrifice and determination that you are victorious. Your gallant courage through these emotional ups and downs have earned you the supreme and unwavering trust of your teammates that will ultimately form powerful bonds that will last forever. With each self-sacrificing achievement of those ten yard's you have acquired unfaltering determination, strategizing skills and abilities to survive the interceptions and fumbles you've experienced to ultimately win—more broadly, to win in life. So, every game on this gridiron of life will take you 10 yards to make that first down, as you then continue on to the next set of downs to ultimately reach that goal line and score. Many of our country's greatest heroes and even some Presidents have played this game. Now, with all of that in mind, how can anyone dislike this game of football? What is there to hate about it, when it teaches those kinds of lessons and when so many people love the game so much that football today is far and away America's favorite sport?

It all sounds so noble and right, the American Spirit exemplified on a patch of green turf 120 yards long by 53 1/3 yards wide. But it all comes at a ferocious cost among its players, both in terms of catastrophic, life-changing injuries and in direct and indirect loss of life; and this is football's dirty little secret.

Although the history of football goes as far back as 1876, the first American Professional Football Association was created in 1920 (which would change its name to the National Football League, or NFL, only two years later), most experts agree that the modern era of American football began with the 1932 playoff game in which the Chicago Bears defeated the Portsmouth Spartans by a score of 9-0 and scoring all of their points in the fourth quarter. However, a year earlier in 1931, an organization known as the American Football Coaches Association (AFCA) initiated its First Annual Survey of Football Fatalities, which the Association has subsequently commissioned every year since right up to today, except for the war year of 1942 when no survey was taken. Today, the AFCA annual survey is conducted by the National Center for Catastrophic Sports Injury Research (NCCSIR), and the data collected and compiled by NCCSIR over the past 90 years—which includes organized youth leagues and high school programs as well as the professional and college levels—are simply shocking and deeply disturbing to say the least.

For example, over the years from 1931 to 1965, there were a total of 609 fatalities due directly to football—that's an average of nearly 18 deaths per year. Not only that, but the vast majority of these fatalities—480 in total—occurred among youth league and middle and high school players! However, over the ensuing decade from 1966 to 1976, the statistics only got worse. Over that 11-year span, there were 226 fatalities—an average of just over 20 deaths per year due directly to football—and once again, the vast majority of these occurred to youth league and high school players—205 deaths total for an average of nearly 19 deaths annually.

Yet decades of significant changes and adjustments to the rules of play, beginning with sweeping changes restricting the "legal" or allowable uses of the head and helmet in tackling or blocking one's opponent instituted in the mid-1970s have done relatively little to solve the problem. The AFCA survey reveals that from 1977 through the 2018 season there were 222 fatalities due directly to football, and once again the vast majority of those—a total of 179—occurred to middle and high school players.

Further, it should be pointed out that NCCSIR defines fatalities due directly to football, which it calls "Direct traumatic injury," as: "Those fatalities which resulted directly from participation in the fundamental skills of football," such as spine fractures or severe head trauma. However, the AFCA survey also tracks a separate category which it calls "Indirect" or "exertional/systemic" fatalities due to football, and which NCCSIR defines as "Those fatalities that are caused by systemic failure as a result of exertion while participating in a football-related activity (e.g., heat stroke, sudden cardiac arrest[1]) or by a complication which was secondary to a non-fatal injury (e.g., infection)."

Regardless, the numbers of indirect fatalities due to football over these same years are just as disturbing and alarming as those due directly to playing the game—in fact, they indicate an even greater overall number of football related deaths. From 1966 through the 2018 season, there were a total of 512 fatalities indirectly due to football across organized youth leagues, middle and high school programs, professional and semi-pro leagues and intercollegiate, of which a whopping 374 occurred tragically among middle and high school players. In fact, over that entire 53-year span, there were between 5 and 18 fatalities in all but four of those years—an average of nearly 10 deaths annually do indirectly to the game of football.

Moreover, there are at least two other significant factors that would indicate that the AFCA survey may be only the tip of the iceberg. By their own admission, NCCSIR acknowledges that while their report "includes data that is reported... by the NCAA, the NFHS [National Federation of State High School Associations], online reports, [medical] colleagues, coaches, and athletic trainers" there are an unknown number of "additional catastrophic football injuries that are not reported to the NCCSIR." The report further states, "[We] acknowledge that not every catastrophic fatality is included in this report."

The second factor that limits the comprehensive accuracy of the survey is that the data only include organized football programs from kids' Pop Warner leagues across the country through high school and collegiate

---

1   I think it is crucial to note that stroke and cardiac arrest can be brought on by direct, traumatic brain injury resulting in the severe disruption of the brain's auto-regulatory functions. This fact became abundantly clear in Preston's case——as he and his doctors struggled to control or minimize the effects of numerous strokes—any one of which—could potentially have killed him after the fact. What this means is that, even within the definitions prescribed by NCCSIR, a certain percentage of the reported "indirect" fatalities may in fact be more accurately defined as "direct" fatalities due to football.

programs and professional leagues culminating with the established pinnacle of the NFL. Unfortunately, there is really no way of knowing how many catastrophic injuries or fatalities occur every year in this country as a result of informal football play—casual play that, in fact, is less likely to be formally regulated or refereed, and in which the participants are much more likely to use improper or ineffective protective equipment—such as outdated or ill-fitting helmets or inadequate shoulder and leg pads—or in some cases to play with little or no protective equipment at all.[2]

Yet with all of that in mind, the NCCSIR data reveal a combined total of 52 fatalities due directly or indirectly to organized football in America over just the four-year span from 2015 through the most recent 2018 season! It moves me to ask: *Is anyone paying attention to this unconscionable situation?*

Yet we are not through. Because there is at least one other category of football-related fatality that must be recognized, and it is arguably the most tragic and heartbreaking category of all, though it also may be the one that is most difficult to tabulate as attributable directly to the game itself. So difficult, in fact, that the NCCSIR annual football injury survey makes no attempt nor has any mechanism for tracking and recording fatalities due to it.

On January 16, 2018, Tyler Hilinski, a promising young quarterback at Washington State University, was found in his room, dead from a self-inflicted gunshot wound, with a suicide note lying next to his lifeless body. Tyler was only 21 years old. Just over a year earlier, on November 30, 2016, James Ransom, a standout Pop Warner football player only 13 years old, committed suicide in his room in his family's home in Southern California. By the time he was 12 years old, James had three years of tackle football under his belt, and he had suffered a diagnosed concussion a year before taking his own life. James had acknowledged to his parents that he had had his "bell rung" many

---

2   A brief search on Wikipedia reveals that throughout North America there are quite a number of well-organized (and presumably incorporated), informal football leagues with new ones being formed all the time. Providing play for thousands of athlete-participants, these organizations presently include: 8 arena/indoor leagues; 18 semi-pro; 5 leagues listed as "developmental"; 13 collegiate/amateur, and 14 women's leagues. Here again, this list does not include thousands more players who become football "weekend warriors" engaging regularly in either tackle or flag football games through very informal (i.e., non-incorporated) leagues. And make no mistake—there are serious injuries that occur as a result of playing flag football too. It is highly doubtful that concussion injuries suffered by the players in these leagues are ever reported to NCCSIR.

times during those years, an expression so cavalierly common among athletes of all ages playing all kinds of contact sports that we tend to forget that having one's "bell rung" almost always denotes a blow to the brain of unknown severity. But what is more to the point, if you are a parent—and even if not—is that you have to ask yourself this confounding question: What could possibly cause a bright young college man of 21 years old, and an energetic, outgoing schoolboy of only 13—both of whom were intelligent kids who had good homes, loving parents, and their entire, very promising lives ahead of them—both to commit suicide?

The answer to that question may be Chronic Traumatic Encephalopathy (CTE), a degenerative brain disease found in people with a history of repetitive brain trauma, football players in particular, owing of course to repeated blows to the head and helmet over the course of play. The first medical evidence of CTE in football players was published in 2005 by Dr. Bennet Omalu, whose story was portrayed in the movie *Concussion* released in 2015. However, most of what is presently known about the condition comes from the research of neuropathologist Dr. Ann McKee, the Chief Neuropathologist for VA Boston Healthcare System, and director of the CTE Center and Neuropathology Core for the Boston University Alzheimer's Disease Center (BUADC).

Briefly, in CTE a protein that neurologists call Tau forms in clumps that progressively spread throughout the brain, killing brain cells as these clumps develop and expand. The Tau protein, by the way, is the same one that builds up in the brains of Alzheimer's patients, and in fact, some clinical pathologists have described CTE sufferers whom they have autopsied as having "the brain of a 75-year-old" or some similar expression. The earliest symptoms of CTE appear to affect the individual's mood and behavior. Some common changes include impulse control problems, aggression, depression, and paranoia, all of which were especially evident in the case of James Ransom and noted by his parents who duly took him to specialists to try to have him treated for various behavioral issues. (James also experienced problems with motor coordination and balance.) As the disease progresses, some patients may experience problems with thinking and memory, including memory loss, confusion, impaired judgment, and eventually progressive dementia.

CTE is perhaps most notably associated with professional NFL players, perhaps in part due to the previously mentioned film *Concussion*. In point of fact, however, it was Dr. McKee's landmark study, published in July of 2017 by the American Medical Association, which found that the incidence of CTE is dramatically higher among football players of all ages than it is believed to be among the general population. Of the 202 football players included in the study, 177 were diagnosed with CTE. Most shockingly of all, of the 111 NFL players included in the study, 110 had CTE—nearly every single one of them!

Most NFL fans today are probably familiar with some of the players who may have committed suicide over the past two decades potentially as a direct result of their suffering with CTE; these include Terry Long, Andre Waters, Shane Dronnet, Dave Duerson, Ray Easterling, "Junior" Seau, and of course, the sensationally horrific case of Aaron Hernandez, who was convicted of murder and later hanged himself with his bed sheets inside his prison cell. Those same fans will also undoubtedly recognize the names of the many other marquee players who have been diagnosed, post mortem, with CTE; they include Dwight Clark, Frank Gifford, John Mackey, Earl Morrel, Adrian Robinson, Kenny Stabler, Bubba Smith, Tommy Nobis and Mike Webster (the player central to the Bennet Omalu story in *Concussion*).[3] Yet a quick google search on Wikipedia reveals a partial list of dozens of other former players who are still living and who are suspected of having CTE, and in 2013 the NFL reportedly reached an undisclosed settlement with over 4,500 former players in a class action lawsuit for concussion-related injuries resulting from their years of playing in the league.

Now, in all fairness, it needs to be acknowledged that the sample in Dr. McKee's seminal study, the one that diagnosed CTE in 110 of 111 former NFL players, was by no means random. To begin with, presently it is only possible to definitively confirm a diagnosis of CTE posthumously through an autopsy of the brain. Second, all of the 202 former (and deceased) players whose families or guardians agreed to allow the necessary autopsies to be performed for the purposes of the study were already suspected to have suffered with CTE

---

3   Despite growing knowledge and media coverage of the damaging psychological and cognitive effects of CTE, the drumbeat of football-related suicides continues in the present day. The most recent case (that we know of) is that of 47-year-old Jason Hairston of the San Francisco 49ers and Denver Broncos, who took his own life on September 4, 2018.

before they died. Nevertheless, such an overwhelming medical finding should set off alarm bells for the parents of every child or young adult playing the game today—and even among the players themselves who are old enough to understand the ramifications. Keep in mind that the NFL subjects included in McKee's survey were all grown men, whose brains therefore were fully developed, even if the damage to their brains had begun when they were playing football as children. Yet we are talking here about kids playing tackle football as young as ages 7 or 8 in Pop Warner leagues on up to the collegiate level when they are generally 18 to 22 years old. Well, most research today indicates that the human brain is not fully developed until at least the age of 23. What might possibly be happening to the brains of these children, which again are not fully developed, as they constantly experience hit after hit after hit to their heads both in practice and in game play? One of the studies coming out of the most recent research provides an answer to this question that is so alarming that every parent and every young football player should know about and take into serious consideration in deciding whether or not to play the game.

Published in February of 2018 in the respected medical journal *Brain*, the study headed up by Dr. Chad Tagge et al. (along with 45 other signatories including concussion and head trauma experts Robert Cantu and Ann McKee; https://academic.oup.com/brain/article/141/2/422/4815697) looked more directly at the underlying mechanisms that may incrementally lead to full-blown concussion injuries (rather than looking specifically at concussion incidents themselves), as well as to a diagnosis of traumatic brain injury and chronic traumatic encephalopathy (CTE), and also sought to learn more about the complex relationships among these disorders. What these researchers found was that, "closed-head impact injuries, *independent of concussive signs,* can induce traumatic brain injury as well as early pathologies and functional sequelae associated with chronic traumatic encephalopathy" (the term "sequelae" in this context refers to a disease or disorder caused by preceding disease or injury to the same individual). It is worth reiterating more succinctly the finding (which I emphasized in italics in the preceding) that "closed-head impact injuries" can cause traumatic brain injury—including CTE—*without an actual concussion or concussions having occurred!* In a short video accompanying the report, one of the study's authors, spokesperson Dr. Lee Goldstein bluntly states, "The main message of this work is that concussion doesn't cause the CTE, but rather *the hit itself, independent of concussion, causes CTE*" (once again, emphasis mine.)

What this means is that some (and very possibly all) young athletes playing football from Pop Warner right through their senior years of college may be experiencing successive, mild traumas to their brains—incidental but repetitive individual injuries that in and of themselves do not rise to the level of "clinical" concussions but which are nonetheless cumulative in their damaging effect, potentially leading to much more serious, pervasive, and permanent traumatic brain injury or disease such as CTE. Stated differently, just because your football-loving child might have the good fortune (so far) of never having suffered (or been diagnosed as suffering) a concussion, that alone does not mean that he or she has not suffered some significant degree of aggregating traumatic brain injury just from the successive and unrelenting hits that are unfortunately an integral and unavoidable part of the game.

Think about that a little more: What this says is that you can't wait for your kid to have a concussion to consider the very real possibility that they are experiencing some degree of progressive brain damage just from playing football. Each individual hit, by itself, might be insignificant in terms of the degree of trauma inflicted; however cumulatively, all of those repetitive hits may eventually cause devastating traumatic brain injury. This is a fact that I believe every parent of a child who wants to play organized football needs to know and to think about very seriously—and that every kid also needs to think about as soon as they are old enough to understand the potential risks they assume as football players.

* * * * *

Any discussion about the inherent health risks of playing organized football would not be complete without some words about the so-called technological advancements that have been made in connection with the ever-improving protective equipment that is now readily available to modern-day football players of all ages. Since I am focusing primarily on traumatic head and brain injury in this book, I want to talk about helmet design in particular. Both the

NFL and the NCAA have from time to time touted the scientific research that has gone into developing the sophisticated design of modern-day football helmets, which allegedly has made them much more effective in protecting players' heads and brains. And indeed, some studies show that these new helmets significantly reduce the risk and incidence of skull fractures resulting from linear impacts to the head. But here is the absurdity of these studies: Most of them compare the safety of wearing the technologically engineered helmet against *not wearing a helmet at all!* Honestly, was it ever really necessary to conduct a study to discover such an obvious conclusion?

But the obvious fact is that few people would disagree with the idea that modern football helmets significantly reduce the risk of skull fractures. But what about the capacity for those same helmets to effectively protect against concussions or traumatic brain injuries?

A study published in 2014 and first presented at the annual conference of the American Academy of Neurology found that even the best and most technologically advanced, current-model football helmets do little or nothing to protect the brain against hits to the side of the head, or due to rotational force, citing these two factors as the most common and most dangerous sources of brain injury and encephalopathy (https://www.aan.com/PressRoom/Home/PressRelease/1241). In fact, and even more disturbing, in conducting 330 tests designed to measure how well the 10 most popular new helmet designs protect the wearer against TBI, the researchers in this study concluded that on average, the helmets "reduced the risk of traumatic brain injury by only 20 percent compared to *not wearing a helmet at all*" (emphasis mine)! (There they go again with that absurd comparison to playing helmetless!)

Furthermore, in what amounts to a stinging indictment, however oblique, of organizations from the NFL and NCAA right on down to high school programs and Pop Warner league officials, the study authors stated, "Alarmingly, the [helmets] that offered the least protection are among the most popular on the field," adding that, "Biomechanics researchers have long understood that rotational forces, not linear forces, are responsible for serious brain damage including concussion, brain injury complications and brain bleeds. Yet generations of football and other sports participants have been under the [mistaken] assumption that their brains are protected by their investment in headwear protection." This is in fact an unequivocal, and dangerously false sense of protection.

Which is to say that the major football organizations in America have routinely failed both to fit players properly with the best helmet designs available and suited to each individual player, and even more basically, they have refused even to acknowledge that even the most sophisticated helmet design in no way guarantees that the wearer will not be at serious risk of traumatic brain injury due directly from playing the game of football. The result is that you have very young players going out to do battle on the gridiron—players who like Preston are already possessed of the idea that they are invincible and impervious to serious injury—now also going out there with an utterly false sense of comfort and security that their football helmets will protect them from everything, from every sort of violent hit or collision that can possibly happen on the field! And that is absolutely not the case. Why are even these technologically sophisticated modern day helmets so completely ineffective?

Dr. Omalu explains that our human head is not structured for the acceleration and deceleration forces from a hit. The brain itself—that is the live brain—as Omalu describes it, is soft like tofu, made up mostly of fat. It is not at all like the "hard" brains we all have seen in movies and documentaries; brains that obviously have been removed from the body and which are treated with chemicals to make them physically harder, whether for research or horror-film entertainment. When the brain has been damaged or swollen from a concussion, Omalu notes, its consistency is more like that of toothpaste. But the softness or paste-like consistency of the brain is not the only issue.

As I described earlier, Dr. Altschuler at Mercy Hospital had likened Preston's numerous brain injuries to a severe case of shaken baby syndrome, because in performing the surgery he found that his brain was bruised all over as a result of being battered around inside his skull, bouncing from front to back and side to side. But he also confirmed that Preston's brain had suffered both rotational acceleration and linear deceleration as a result of the violent hit that ultimately caused his second impact syndrome. In rotational acceleration, the brain actually turns unnaturally inside the skull, creating powerful angular momentum that literally shears the axons—the crucially important brain cells that connect the various parts of the brain to each other—causing them to tear or completely rupture. Linear deceleration is the phenomenon in which the brain keeps moving after the hit until it smashes against the boney-hard insides of the skull and bounces around. Severe linear deceleration also shears or ruptures the critical arteries leading to brain, often resulting in multiple brain bleeds as well as catastrophically cutting off oxygen to the brain. And of course, all of this violently destructive action occurs inside the skull, so it ought to be quite clear that there is no form of external protection on earth, helmet or otherwise, that is even remotely capable of preventing it from happening.

The bottom line for Ted and me is that Preston's helmet did not prevent him from suffering the first concussion in practice drills, and as the game film clearly shows, in the game against Duquesne, his helmet wasn't even a factor in the second hit that resulted in his severe brain trauma and nearly ended his life. Those two facts ought to comprise a cautionary tale for any parents of children playing the game of football, as well as the young athletes themselves.

* * * * *

Throughout this chapter we have taken a hard and unflinching look at the dangerous and potentially deadly, dark side of the game of football, and organized football in particular. This chapter has revealed some very disturbing statistics about the game's long and continuing history of fatalities due both directly and indirectly to on-field play or practice, as well as the tragic issue of player suicides that may be connected to repeated concussions and long-term traumatic brain injury. We have also looked at a number of scientific medical research studies that prove the link between playing football and TBI and CTE.

Yet, I think you will agree that I began this chapter with a fairly glowing and venerating, almost philosophical description of the game of football and the life lessons it imparts; those of teamwork and fairness and personal responsibility, of building self-confidence and determination in one's pursuit of success in both life and career, to name but a few—qualities that I honestly do believe athletic competition imparts to young people and contributes to their maturation as adults. In spite of all that has happened to my boy Preston and my family, I do still somewhat like the game in all its facets and intricacies, and I recognize that football is nothing short of massively entertaining to many. So, honestly, it is not my purpose in this book to bash the game of football to death, or to call for its abolishment on any level, or anything of that sort. My intention is to do my best to educate and bring to the forefront the dangers and consequences of this beloved American sport so that athletes, coaches, trainers, parents and organizations can more honestly address the risks involved, and to provide and maintain a strict and watchful attentiveness to protect these young precious brains.

However, what I have come to hate about the game, especially in the aftermath of Preston's injury, has been the far too common failure and the sheer unwillingness on the part of the game's many proponents—the NFL and NCAA in particular—to acknowledge the inherent and unavoidable risks of very serious, life-changing and even life-ending consequences of playing the game, and to be completely transparent and forthcoming to the general public about the risks—not to mention to the players themselves.

When Jeff Miller, the NFL's senior vice president for health and safety, while appearing at a roundtable discussion on concussions convened by the U.S. House of Representatives' Committee on Energy and Commerce in March of 2016, openly acknowledged that there is "certainly" a link between football and neurodegenerative diseases like CTE, his stunning admission made national headlines. That's because the NFL had previously, categorically, denied the existence of any such connection, and even when league officials were forced by growing and overwhelming evidence (and intense pressure from both players and the public) to soften their rigid stance, they said that they would leave it up to the professional medical community to determine if there was a link. Often it took a major tragedy and public outcry to effect any change, for example, in the rules of play. That's a fact that hits home for me and my family, because it wasn't until after Preston's devastating, life-long injury—and to a large measure *because* of Preston's injury and the subsequent lawsuit—that the NCAA began a serious review of its then woefully deficient rules determining when and under what circumstances athletes may return to play following concussions—rules that could have saved Preston from the debilitating SIS he suffered and must live with the rest of his life.

Fortunately today, football organizations on many levels seem to be headed in the right direction. In the wake of Jeff Miller's admission on Capitol Hill, the NFL issued a statement in which it pledged $100 million to support "independent medical research and engineering advancements in neuroscience related topics," which the league claimed was "in addition to the $100 million that the NFL and its partners are already spending on medical and neuroscience research." And indeed, from 2002 through 2017, the NFL instituted more than 47 rule changes to protect players, improve practice methods, and better educate players and personnel on concussion injuries. More recently, as any NFL fan knows, the league has established a game-time, sideline medical examination protocol for immediately identifying and diagnosing on-field concussions and other head-related injuries and removing injured players from the game. And while my main concern, to be perfectly honest, is for the college and high school athletes, and the youngest kids in Pop Warner-type leagues, it is critically important that the NFL steps up and takes the lead in this effort. Because what the NFL acknowledges, and the actions it takes in response, all tends to filter down through the entire system.

* * * * *

Box 8.1. Comparing Modern Football Helmets Against 1930's "Leatherheads: A Ridiculous Laboratory Experiment? — Or Maybe Not?

Every now and then from the annals of medical science research, there comes a study that seems bizarrely conceived, even absurd to the point where you find yourself scratching your head and asking, *What were these people thinking about?* But here's an intriguing and very illuminating story. One such very recent study actually compared the impact properties of modern plastic helmets against a selection of the old, original "leatherhead" helmets, many of which were 80 years old, in which the leather was brittle and cracking from age! The authors of this seemingly ridiculous study, published in 2013 in the respected *Journal of Neurosurgery* no less, had the audacity to conclude (apparently seriously) that the modern plastic helmets reduce the risk of concussions by 45 to 96 percent over the old leather crafted models (Rowson, Daniel, & Duma, 2013)! Here again, any rational person ought rightly to expect that the highly sophisticated, technologically/scientifically advanced, molded high-strength plastic and rubber-foam helmet models of today should without any question whatsoever provide far superior skull and brain protection compared against the nearly century-old "vintage" leather helmets from back in the day when the Ford Model T was the most popular car on the American road. The comparison is almost comical—one thinks of images showing The Three Stooges or the Bowery Boys haphazardly wearing the floppy leather models on their heads playing the game knee deep on some muddy gridiron were the issue and its ramifications not so deadly serious. So why would any respected medical researchers even conduct such a seemingly pointless and idiotic study?

Well, it turns out that the Rowson (2013) study was published apparently in response to a similar study conducted barely one year earlier and also published in the *Journal of Neurosurgery*. In stark contrast, however, that previous study (Bartsch, Benzel, Miele, & Prakash, 2013) found virtually *no difference whatsoever* between the concussive protective properties of either the modern plastic and the original leather models, the authors going so far as to report astoundingly that in some instances the protection afforded by "wearing vintage leatherheads [was] *comparable to or better than* [that] while wearing several widely used 21st century varsity helmets." In other words, in some of the impact tests used in the study, the leather helmets actually outperformed the plastic ones! Yet how do we explain such conflicting findings between these two studies? The answer is very simple, and it is profoundly instructive.

Rowson and his colleagues had conducted very unsophisticated linear-impact tests in which a simulated human "dummy" head, fitted with each of the different football helmets to be tested, was dropped onto a hard, flat surface from various distances and at various angles. Whereas Bartsch and his colleagues had created a more sophisticated model in which they tested a helmeted head form striking a second helmeted head form that was mounted on a flexible neck, permitting linear and rotational head motion. This model enabled them to simulate direct-front, oblique-front, oblique-rear, and direct-rear head impacts in order to induce concussive head impact forces on par with approximately the 95th percentile of on-field collision severity, the researchers noting that, "In the real world, American Football collisions always involve combinations of linear and rotational motion."

In a later editorial critical of Rowson's findings, Bartsch and his colleagues pointed out that the flaw in the Rowson (2013) study was that the standard, straight-line drop test these researchers employed was originally designed only to determine how well different football helmet models protect the wearer against suffering a *skull fracture*—not concussive traumatic brain injury. Bartsch asserted that Rowson's results proved nothing more than "one's skull would be significantly better protected [against fracture] when running headfirst into a brick wall while wearing a modern American football helmet versus a vintage leather helmet."

Well, that's a relief!

CHAPTER 9

RISING TO THE CHALLENGES
AND COMING HOME

"Thou art the God that doest wonders:
thou hast declared thy strength among the people."

— Psalm 77:14

I can honestly say that we were not a family that went to church faithfully every Sunday. We would attend once in a while for the social aspect, for example, participating in the Parish bowling league and volunteering during the annual carnival and other church functions. However, going to church was mandatory during the traditional holidays, especially at Christmas with its captivating music, sense of community, the comforting feeling of tradition, and possibly even some guilt. Many would consider us as "Chreastain's," or "Chreaster's": people that attend church twice on the two holiest days of the Christian year, Christmas and Easter. But this did not mean that I was not spiritual. Rather, I just did not believe that I had to go to church to connect with God. However, Christmas to me always held a special "magical power"; that enchanting season that could transport me back to the delightful feelings of my own childhood wonderment. I remember one Christmas Eve when

Preston and Perry were young, when just as we were exiting the church after the Midnight Mass, it started to snow. I looked at the boys and said with so much delight; "Look boys, it's snowing! Santa, is on his way!" Their eyes danced with excitement, their youthful faith and imagination igniting my own childhood memories of this magical holiday and arousing an exciting renewal of hope, joy, and a peaceful sense that all was well.

In my profound distress over Preston's dire situation, I desperately sought out that divine magical power and prayed so hard to God every day to be blessed with a miracle. Countless people have benefited from miracles, and certainly many books have been written and movies made telling powerful stories of recovery that the most advanced medical science cannot explain. Nevertheless, my prayers during these times were constant day and night, and indeed Preston did appear, slowly, to make some incremental progress. However, there was no denying the fact that he was not the same Preston that we all knew before the injury. I found myself at times peering into his eyes, and for the life of me I could not find him; I could not find that energetic, charismatic, and strong inner soul as I knew him. "Where are you Preston?" I would implore, fighting back weary tears. "Fight Preston! Fight hard! Find that extraordinary inner spirit of yours and fight your way back!" I would plead with a frustrated, shattered heart. More than ever, I tried to be hopeful and faithful and pray that Preston would be granted the miraculous divine healing power and bring him from his place of darkness and back into the light. In utter desperation and despair, I humbly requested, I shamelessly bargained, and I mercifully begged my Lord God for this miracle, but I would eventually find my visions of a miracle would be very different from God's.

Yet, when I think back about the long and arduous six months that Preston was in JFK Hospital and the Children's Specialized Rehabilitation facility, my recollections are a cascading kaleidoscope of emerging circumstances and unforeseen events—both positive and, well, not so positive—that all seem to run together in my memory like different colored sand simultaneously draining through an hourglass. It was also a time during which we seemed to be called upon to make one heart-wrenching decision after another with regard to Preston's ongoing care and treatment, as he seemed to face one complication or obstacle after another.

Preston remained in JFK hospital through all of December of 2005 and all of January of 2006. Any progress being welcome, no matter how incremental, it was there that his first monumental and exciting advancement would begin. That occurred when he moved his left leg for the first time—breaking free of his quadriplegic symptoms signifying that he would eventually walk again—and at last opened his eyes. It was also at JFK that cognitive tests confirmed that Preston had emerged from the coma that had gripped him since the injury. Such clinical tests are what they are, but the fact was that even with the coma behind him, Preston was still massively impaired both physically and mentally, and the only physical movements we got from him in response to questions were eye movements and an occasional thumb's up. Those raised thumbs were heartening nevertheless, because they indicated that Preston's spirits were still up. With these improvements came the moment where we were taken into that bleak conference room and once again told it was time to move Preston into a long-term rehab hospital.

When he was at last moved to Children's Specialized Hospital on January 30th and placed into their in-house rehabilitation facility, Preston was still unable to hold himself up, stand, or walk and was therefore wheelchair-bound. However, we were excited and hopeful as Preston was finally given a therapy routine everyday consisting of Physical Therapy, Occupational Therapy, Speech Therapy, and Pool Therapy just to name a few. In time, he did begin to move his left arm in using a communication board in order to "talk" to us, but it was at Children's that Preston was diagnosed with Apraxia of Speech (AOS). AOS is a speech sound disorder in which the patient has trouble saying what he or she wants to say correctly and consistently. The National Institutes of Health (NIH) describes AOS as a neurological disorder that affects the brain pathways involved in planning the sequence of movements involved in producing speech, adding that the brain knows what it wants to say, but cannot properly plan and sequence the required speech sound movements. Even with this devastating affliction, with which he still struggles today, we were overjoyed that he was cognitive, that he could slowly process information, think, and that he was aware of his surroundings.

As you might imagine for starters, Preston's hospitalization completely disrupted our family's normal routine, particularly as Ted and I were determined that we would never leave Preston alone—that one of us would be at his bedside at all times, night and day. I will always be enormously grateful to Children's for their policy allowing parents to stay overnight with their sons or daughters as often and as regularly as they wanted to.

So, as Ted continued to go to his job during the workweek, I stayed with Preston, literally running my own business from a laptop computer at my son's bedside. Ted would often stop by in the morning and bring me coffee and breakfast on his way to work, or he would visit Preston and me in the early evenings on his homeward trip. Then, after five weekdays of tending to Preston, Ted would take over on Friday night, staying with Preston for the weekend so that I could go home and spend much needed time with Perry when he was home, and just relax a bit and unwind. I would return first thing Monday morning for another week and then repeat. This was our unrelenting family routine for the six months that Preston remained at Children's Hospital. On my 40-minute drive home on Friday nights, I found this to be the best time for me to talk to God. I would plead again and again for God's graces for a miracle. I could not understand, if God's ear is open to my prayers, and I'm praying diligently, why was there such little evidence of His answering?" So often during these trips back home when Preston was struggling with difficult times I would grab the steering wheel so hard and scream at the top of my lungs; "Whyyyyyyyy!" Why did this awful tragedy happen? Why do you not hear my prayers for a miracle? I need your strength." Exhausted in defeat I lessen to a final soft whimper, "Help my son."

In addition to the standard therapies, the doctors and therapists would also apply other various strategies and methods including medications to facilitate Preston's recovery and ultimately to gradually restore his independence. One Friday in particular proved to be stressful at every turn. Preston had endured more pain and anguish than I would have wished upon my worst enemy. During these times of suffering I would sometimes become, as a mother, both suspicious and skeptical with regard to the methods used to try to support his recovery. So for example, due to the numerous strokes he had suffered, Preston's right arm started to show signs of spasticity in which the muscles began to contract involuntarily. This caused his right arm to bend at the elbow, drawing the forearm slowly upwards until it rested on his upper chest, where it would remain immobilized if not treated, while also making the fingers of his righthand curl tightly underneath as if grasping a pole. This spasticity occurs as a result of damage to the portion of the brain or spinal cord that controls voluntary movement, and a procedure called Casting Immobilization was used to correct it before it would become uncorrectable and permanent. Preston was first given Botox injections to relax the muscles, and then a hard cast, pushing his arm down slightly, was placed on the arm extending from his shoulder all the way down to his hand. After a few days the cast was removed and a new cast was positioned to force his arm down a bit more, and this process would continue until eventually his arm would be all the way back down to his side.

To their credit, Children's Specialized Hospital was always on top of the latest and most effective procedures to help promote the best possible recovery outcomes, and yet, while this procedure would turn out to be very successful for Preston, forcing Preston's arm "back into position" this process had all the enlightened appearance of some brutal medical treatment from the asylums of the Dark Ages. In fact, the method was by no means perfect, and it occurred during the long procedure that there was one position that clearly put Preston into severe pain. When I told the doctor and nurses that something was wrong, they responded rather matter-of-factly that he was just experiencing some discomfort because the new cast was pushing his arm down to a new, lower position. This did sound plausible; however, this was not the first time a new cast was put on, and he had not responded in this way to any of the previous castings. This one was different.

So, I adamantly persisted—relentlessly. "Something is wrong, and the cast needs to be removed!"

Sure enough, the next day after taking lunch, I returned to Preston's room to find that he was not there, and I asked a nurse where he was. She said, "Preston was taken to the casting room to have the cast removed." Quickly as I could, I got to the casting room just as the technician was removing the cast, revealing that Preston's arm was an alarming combination of dark purple and blue. "Oh my God!" I shouted. "What happened to his arm? I told you something was wrong, why did you wait?" I exclaimed. My anger was intense, and a nurse grabbed me and took me to a private room where I met with Dr.

Krishan Yalamanchi. who explained that a small bone fracture had occurred in Preston's hand caused by the casting, and it was this fracture that was causing him the pain.

What had actually happened was that the casting had inadvertently re-fractured his earlier hand injury from football—the same one that had required a steel pin to fix! Thus, football again had raised its ugly head to bestow one last insulting blow. However, the crucial lesson I realized from this incident is the importance of a family advocate in these hospital situations. As parents we all are advocates for our children to varying degrees, but when your family member has a medical crisis, advocacy takes on a whole new level and significance. Preston could not talk, his processing was extremely slow, he was unable to communicate his needs, and especially his pain. As a mother I knew something was wrong, I saw it in his eyes, felt it in my heart and patiently questioned him, and then I spoke up for him—loudly. Who knows how long he would have suffered before that cast came off if I were not there to advocate for him. So, you must become their voice speaking for your loved one, but also by informing hospital personnel, from nurses and aides to technicians and doctors, to understand both their physical and emotional necessities based on your intimate communicative connection with that loved one. You do not need a medical license or a background in healthcare, but your voice, your loving and caring presence significantly matters not only to your loved one, but also to the hospital staff who will also benefit in doing their jobs with your guidance.

The ordeal of the spasticity in Preston's right arm is only one example among so many, in his semi-comatose state, in which physically harsh methods had to be used to help his body to fight off the ever-present danger of severe muscle atrophy that threatened to become permanent if allowed to progress. While sleeping at night, for another example, either Ted or I had to strap large plaster casts tightly onto both of his feet and lower legs right up to just below the knees. Looking exactly like the casts you see on someone who has suffered a broken leg, Preston had to wear these heavy immobilizing contraptions while he slept every night to prevent from developing footdrop. Can you imagine trying to sleep restfully or comfortably with two huge, hard casts, like a couple of giant ski boots, weighing down both of your legs? Then add the full cast on his arm, it was painful just having to watch this and imagine what it must have been like for him.

* * * * *

Rehabilitation

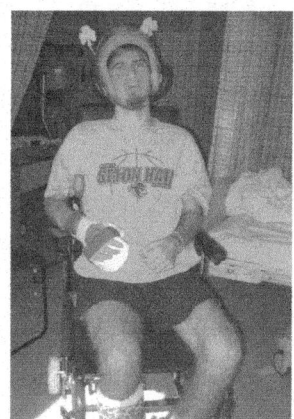

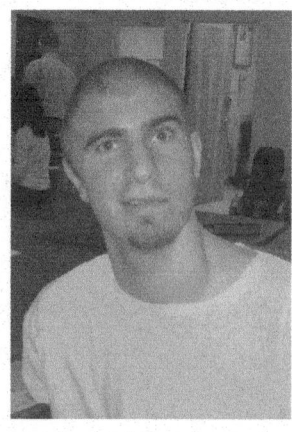

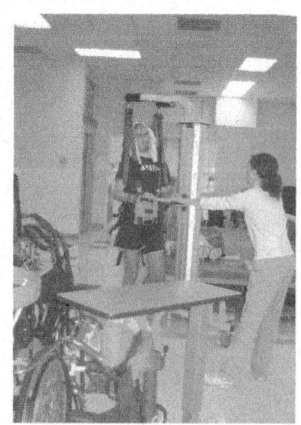

Albert Einstein once said, "There are only two ways to live your life. One is as though nothing is a miracle. The other is as if everything is." While relentlessly praying for that big miracle, small miracles were happening all the time, encouraging us to not stop believing. In February a remarkable thing happened, which nonetheless came about ironically as a result of a different family tragedy when we lost my grandmother to Alzheimer's. Having battled that devastating disease for many years, her passing was not unexpected, and it was really one of those cases, sadly, where we could at least take some solace from knowing that she was finally at peace.

Of course, I had to inform the hospital and rehab staff that I would be gone for a couple of days to attend the funeral. This was particularly important because I had taken on much of Preston's essential daily caregiving, and I wanted to make sure his needs would continue to be met during my absence; I didn't want him falling through the cracks once again. So, at one point while Preston was in physical therapy, I pulled the therapist off to the side to explain the situation to her quietly and confidentially.

Suddenly, sitting in his wheelchair off by the weight machines, Preston began to cry uncontrollably, much to my surprise.

Preston does not show any emotion during this time. This is a common symptom after a TBI referred to as "flat affect" where normal emotions are absent. It doesn't mean that he doesn't have feelings, it just means that his brain and body have a hard time translating an emotion into a physical reaction. So, my immediate thought was that he was in some kind of physical pain, so I immediately went over to him, bent down and asked, "Preston are you in any pain?" I pulled the communication board out of the back pocket of his wheelchair and placed it on his lap so that he could tell me what was wrong. With agonizingly slow movements of his left hand, he slowly spelled out: *How – did – she – die?* An anguished, distraught sensation raced through my body as I became painfully aware that he had overheard my conversation with the therapist! There was nothing wrong with his hearing; that was for sure!

"Preston, she was very sick," I started to explain solemnly. Yet nothing I said seemed to stop him from crying, so we decided to end the therapy session right there and I wheeled him back to his room. I could not understand for the life of me why he was taking this so hard. The plain fact was, he did not really know my grandmother all that well; throughout most of his life she had been residing in a hospital for Alzheimer's patients that was located over three hundred miles from our home. Consequently, he hardly ever saw her. So, I was deeply perplexed as to what was causing this uncontrollable outbreak of sorrow, and where on earth this rush of deep anguish was coming from.

Once back in his room and after Preston had composed himself a bit, I gave him back his communication board and pleaded, "Please tell me why you are so sad." Emotionally drained at this point, and even a little physically exhausted as well, he slowly dragged his left index finger from one letter to the next as he spelled out: *How – did – grandma – die?*

"What?" I exclaimed as the stunning realization hit me like a bright beam of light that abruptly began to deflate my fear and anxiety.

Oh my God, that's it! I now understood exactly what was wrong.

I grabbed my oldest son and gave him a big hug and then drawing back with both my hands on his boney shoulders, looked directly into his tearful eyes and said, "Preston, do you think grandma died?" Immediately he began to wail again, and I grabbed him one more time in a tight hug and said, "Oh my dear boy, your grandma did not die, mine did! Your grandmother is still alive!" I was overjoyed that I had found the reason for his outburst, but for some reason he would not stop crying. *Maybe he didn't believe me,* I reasoned, perhaps thinking that I was lying to him just to make him feel better.

While in that quintessential moment I was heartbroken that he was so distraught, I was at the same time indescribably euphoric that Preston had just displayed a profoundly emotional reaction for the very first time since his injury. The pain he was feeling was clearly coming from his heart and mind rather than from the simply physical, and it was the most hopeful, humanly passionate reaction I had witnessed from him right up until that moment. Even more exciting was the fact that he was exhibiting memory that was clearly still intact. Was his brain healing? Was Preston coming out of his unknowable darkness and fighting his way back home? This was an incredible moment in which I was met with such hopeful exhilaration that I can hardly describe it in words. You have to understand that this was really the first time we were able to know, as harsh as it sounds to say it, that Preston was still "in there"; that he was aware of what was going on, that he was aware of his own self, and that he was fully aware of who we were. It is interesting to note that the word "miracle" comes from the Latin word meaning "something wonderful," and in our case this little miracle was indeed something wonderful. It is now that I am humbly reminded that every prayer is heard but God chooses to answer them in His own way and in His own time, even if His responses are small.

However, I did not have time to think about this incredible development right at that moment; Preston was in emotional distress, and I needed to calm him down—I needed to convince him that his beloved grandmother was still quite alive and well. So I wiped away the tears from his face and said, "Let's call grandma so you can hear her voice, okay?"

Have you ever had a moment in your life when you absolutely, positively needed someone to answer their phone and for some unknowable reason they did not answer your call?! This was that dreadful, agonizing moment for me. I called my mom again and again to no avail, so I finally left an urgent message to call me back as soon as possible. Fortunately, she did so only about five minutes later.

"Mom," I said eagerly yet tenderly, "I'm here with Preston and I need you to talk to him and tell him you are alive and well."

Understandably bewildered, she stammered, "What? What in the world are you talking about?"

I explained to her what had just transpired and that Preston believed that it was she who had died instead of her own mother, my grandmother. "Oh no," she replied. "Put him on and I'll talk to him."

I put the phone up to his ear and watched with relief as his tears subsided and contentment erased the misery of his grief as he listened to my mom. Serenity finally set in replacing his anguish with a gratified smile signaling all was well. When I got back on the phone with my mom I said to her, "How incredible this experience was for you to witness how a loved one would react to the announcement of your death." Not everyone gets to witness the expression of love and grief coming from a loved one and should be a lesson never forgotten. The poet Helen Steiner Rice once said, "There's a lot of comfort in the thought that sorrow, grief and woe are sent into our lives sometimes to help our souls to grow."

* * * * *

One of the hardest realities we had to face while Preston was in Children's was the fact that, one way or another, his skull would have to be restored or closed up in order for us to finally be able to bring him safely home. The reason that reality was so difficult is that we were obliged to make a rather excruciating decision about whether to have the surgeons restore the actual bone flap, which remained stored in a lab at Mercy Hospital back in Pittsburgh, or to go with a synthetic prosthetic replacement. While many experts in the medical profession believe that restoring the original bone flap, called cranioplasty, is the option that offers the best prospects for restoring natural cerebral blood flow and, according to one source (http://www.npplweb.com/wjsr/full-text/5/5), "may improve neurological function by recovering cerebrospinal fluid (CSF) dynamics" (Acciarri, Nicolini, & Martinoni, 2016), there is however a very serious and dangerous downside to this seemingly obvious and comfortably intuitive choice.

Specifically, that same study found that the complication rate for cranioplasty ranges as high as a whopping 41 percent of cases, due mainly to potentially serious infections resulting from the surgical procedure. In addition, and particularly distasteful (I would say absolutely hideously distasteful) to think about doing to my son, who had already been through so much, cranioplasty of the natural bone flap requires more extensive scraping away of scar tissue that naturally forms around the perimeter of the open skull so that the bone flap may be better "fitted" back into place. Moreover, it is this scraping away of scar tissue that contributes most significantly to the risk of complication due to infection. The risk of life-threatening infection had been a constantly overriding and greatly worrisome concern since the day Preston was injured, especially because of the damage that had occurred to the parts of his brain that control the body's natural auto-immune systems. Bluntly stated, just about any normally mild infection could potentially kill him in his compromised state.

With an implant solution, a pre-operative high-resolution computer tomography scan would be taken of the area, including all the scarring, thus providing the ideal cranial implant to be fit perfectly without the need to scrape away scar tissue and risk any infection. So, when all was said and done, we opted for the 3D prefabricated cranial prosthetic, and we proceeded to schedule the surgery to be performed by neurosurgeon Dr. Saadi Ghatan at New York's Columbia Presbyterian Hospital, sometime around the middle of March, although the exact date escapes me today.

That is in part because, somewhat ironically, it was a common but potentially serious infection that would delay for nearly a month the surgery to implant the prosthetic section into Preston's head. As anyone familiar with hospitals knows, they are actually the best places in the world (or the worst, depending on your perspective) for acquiring unwanted and often troublesome, recalcitrant infections, of which in degree and variety, hospitals are virtual storehouses. In this regard Preston was no different than any other patient, and somewhere along the way, and likely very early during his long hospitalization, he had contracted the infection known as *Clostridium difficile,* often called C. diff for short.

C. diff is a bacterium that can cause a range of gastro-intestinal illnesses with symptoms ranging from extremely abnormal and extremely foul-smelling diarrhea to life-threatening inflammation of the colon, or colitis. I can't tell you how many cans of air-freshener I went through and it was still not enough to mask this horrific odor. C. diff is actually quite common, with an estimated 200,000 cases annually in the U.S. alone, but a potentially very dangerous infection (and just to reiterate—especially dangerous to Preston given his body's chronically deficient immunological state) that often results, in yet another irony, from the disruption of healthy bacteria in the colon caused but the use of doctor-prescribed antibiotics. That explains why C. diff is so common in hospitals, where dozens upon dozens of patients pop antibiotic pills like candy from a Pez dispenser. Then of course, you have any number of nurses, doctors, technicians, orderlies, visitors, and everybody else going in and out of patients' rooms spreading all sorts of infections to every surface or instrument they touch! For Dr. Ghatan to do the delicate surgery, Preston had to be free of any known bacterial infections.

Accordingly, the doctors at Children's had attempted repeatedly to clear the C. diff infection through the prescribed, by-the-book treatment that called for the use of either of two very powerful antibiotics once a day for a precise period not to exceed ten days. In fact, these antibiotics (Vancomycin and Flagyl) are so potent that there is a medical limit on how many times the 10-day treatments could be applied—three times only, for each of the two strong antibiotics currently in use. None of the treatments worked. Preston would appear to be cured at the end of ten days, but inevitably it seemed, the C. diff infection would soon reemerge. Not only that, but he was quickly running out of permitted 10-day treatment regimens; by the time he was due to undergo the surgery, he had exhausted his three allowable tries on the one medication, and he was on the third and final try with the second antibiotic, and we were quite worried.

On the day we brought Preston to New York for the surgery, and upon discovering that he still had c-diff, a very angry Dr. Ghatan scared the daylights out of us when he declared, shouting, "I can't operate! He's still infected!" Whereupon the neurosurgeon took over direct charge of Preston's treatment by ordering that he be kept on the second antibiotic for 20 straight days rather than ten. Dr. Ghatan's order for the extended treatment worked at last, and the surgery to close Preston's skull with a prosthetic implant was successfully performed—of all days—on Good Friday, April 14th, 2006. Nor did this surgery come without its ups and downs, as Preston's still-injured brain would again swell, causing him to temporarily slip back into a state of cognitive unawareness or semi-unconsciousness once again. Afterwards, Preston started to gradually become more alert, but he still could not walk or talk, and he would demonstrate difficulty with swallowing that still troubles him to this day, particularly when he must swallow his many essential medications. In any event, it would be another six weeks of intensive physical therapy, to try to get him ready for a non-hospital environment, before we could finally bring Preston home, which finally happened during the Memorial Day weekend at the end of May.

As exciting and fulfilling, as simultaneously exhilarating and horrifically frightening the triumph of transition occurring that day was, bringing Preston from impersonal hospital to loving home—for all of the unknowable unknowns that Preston, Ted, Perry, and I faced as a family—the day was not without considerable and ominous foreboding and uncertainty. Because in the weeks leading up as the great day approached, the nurses recommended that we start introducing Preston to some of the very normal things he would encounter "on the outside" (as I write this, it sounds like I'm talking more about someone getting out of prison, yet I think that Preston carries his own personal prison around with him all of his waking hours).

Of course, one of the most basic things that had to happen, was that Preston had to be weaned off the feeding tube that had been used to provide his nourishment since day one of his injury, and encouraged, or retrained if you will, to eat solid food once again. Preston was diagnosed with Oropharyngeal Dysphagia, a swallowing condition resulting from the neurological damage he sustained from the brain injury and subsequent strokes. This condition weakens the throat muscles, making it difficult to move the food down the throat and esophagus when swallowing. This can cause gagging, coughing or in Preston's case, choking.

So, on one occasion, for the first time we gave him a serving of his favorite crispy chicken nuggets from one of those famous fast-food establishments, which we presented to him with much of the fanfare that you would momentously present someone with a birthday cake. Preston happily popped one of those little morsels into his mouth and literally began choking to death. The code blue alarm was initiated and a legion of white coats rushed to his bedside pushing me aside as I stood helplessly in the corner scared and praying that this little piece of chicken would not be his final demise after all he had triumphantly gotten through. Fortunately, the nugget was successfully removed, and I gratefully watched the color of life return to his body as he resumed breathing normally, and death was once again averted. To this day Preston still struggles with swallowing food and even taking liquids, which keeps us on our toes at all times.

Nearly every single day during his seven months in hospital and rehabs, Preston faced significant, often formidable medical, mental, and physical challenges, one after another, that are too numerous and too complicated to detail all of them in this book, and so in this chapter I have only described a few of them. Yet, on seeing a near-disaster with a small piece of a chicken nugget, I started to wonder and worry: how many other common things around our house, or in our refrigerator, or in our garage, or out in the yard or the street—how many of these were going to pose risky dangers to Preston's health and safety; to his very life? And how ready were Ted and I to undertake the profound and massive responsibility of taking care of our oldest son's every need 24/7, from personal hygiene to physical therapy to… well, to promoting his continued maturation as a human being, to the extent of what was possible?

Box 9.1 BAND OF BROTHERS

> *"Two are better than one because they have a good return for their labor. For if either of them falls, the one will lift up his companion. But woe to the one who falls when there is not another to lift him up. Furthermore, if two lie down together they keep warm, but how can one be warm alone?"*

—Ecclesiastes 4:9-12

From the cold and gloomy day in mid-November when he entered Kessler to the May Memorial Day weekend when he finally came home, I can say categorically that there was not a single day over the course of that nearly seven-month stretch on which Preston did not have at least one visitor, and usually several, who came to see him either individually or in groups.

That streak would have begun at Mercy Hospital in Pittsburgh, had the doctors allowed it. Preston's teammates, from both college and high school but especially from high school, all wanted to see him. They were concerned and confused and, I think, a little frightened by the whole thing. I could see it in the eyes of the young men I met in Preston's hospital rooms: this catastrophic injury had clearly shaken many of them. However, the doctors at Mercy felt that allowing too many visitors would be too much for Preston and advised against it, and in his physically compromised state, that was probably for the best.

Yet I could fully understand why they would want to see him, he belonged to that group of young men dedicated and loyal to the game of football—but even more intensely dedicated to each other—the Band of Brothers. I asked the coaches to please ask the boys to pray for Preston and his speedy recovery, and in response among other things, these young men, these brothers, along with the entire student body and faculty of La Salle University came together and held a vigil for him at the Philadelphia campus over 300 hundred miles away from Mercy Hospital. Devastated that we were unable to attend, wanting only to be by Preston's side in his time of greatest need, we were nevertheless completely humbled by LaSalle's divine gesture.

How wonderful these boys are, this tight-knit band of brothers. Yet in many ways I can only marvel at the close bond that exists among them. That's because for me, growing up in a military family, we were constantly on the move to a new base in a new city, and I never had sufficient time to really develop a truly deep, longtime friendship. I never allowed myself to get close to anyone because I did not want to feel that pain and disappointment when inevitably I had to leave.

I have always admired the friendships that I saw develop between my sons and their athlete friends and teammates. Maybe Teddy Roosevelt and Knute Rockne, and all the others who liked to claim that football builds character, were right to a degree. While football undeniably embodies certain negative aspects of aggression and violence, I have come to find that football also embodies many positive qualities as well, and I am talking most particularly about the Band of Brothers a brotherhood that binds teammates together, and which makes them loyal friends for life.

It seems clear that nothing builds more profound friendships among men than the shared, intensive, everyday training and the all-consuming brutal action of a great and magnificent battle. However, there is also the evident warmth and compassion towards one another during these games as displayed through those gestures like the high-fives, the bewildering custom of slaps on the butt, and even "manly" hugs that bring joy and happiness not only to the teammates, but also to the legions of admiring fans in the grandstands. I imagine that is why the band of brothers in football as well as in other sports appears to transcend all other friendships. Once these relationships are consummated, a process that seems to begin right from the very first time these teammates don their uniforms and set foot on the field of play, the bonds are virtually unbreakable for life, or so it seems. Success on the fields depends on mutual respect and cooperation, and as a team, the players create these special friendships, one imagines, because of the trust they must build through the heavy physical price they must pay to win.

In his burning desire to be a part of the game, Preston paid the highest price with his life. But Preston also believed passionately in the ideals of loyalty and kinship that are the heart and soul of the Band of Brothers, symbolizing that belief with a band tattooed around his upper left arm. I believe that Preston intimately embraced these timeless values and ideals that so transcend the game itself. In fact I know he still does, and that remains an integral part of who he is today. That is why he does not blame the game of football for his tragic injury, only the ignorance that for far too long has surrounded certain aspects of it, like the failure of the game's proponents to fully grasp the potential risk of traumatic brain injury, or to understand the dire consequences of not requiring sufficient time to heal a concussive head injury just like one very normally would for a broken arm or leg.

Most important of all, the powerful allegiance and shining loyalty of this brotherhood manifests well beyond the practice fields and the game-day stadiums and the sweaty locker rooms to a deep interpersonal concern for one's comrades, especially when a warrior goes down. I personally witnessed this warmth and compassion taken to a new level towards Preston when he got hurt. A gladiator, a warrior, a brother, had sacrificed and fallen, and because it could have been any one of them, desertion was simply not an option. For seven months they rallied to his hospital bedside.

To this day, so many years later after the injury, while his teammates from college have moved on, his close high school teammates—these boys that became men together—still to this day come out to visit with Preston, most particularly on Super Bowl Sunday. Through social media his coaches from high school and college also still keep in touch with him as well. But was it only football, and his prowess on the field that was so special about Preston?

No, not at all. When Preston was injured, hundreds of people posted messages on his Facebook wall or sent him emails conveying their well-wishes. From these posts I discovered a different Preston than the one I knew at home. I learned that he was funny, smart (street-smart, maybe), kind, fair-minded, and yes, even humble in his own sort of way. Far from the kid I knew who paraded his godly swagger all around our home. Did I ever really know who the real Preston was? I discovered that inside that loud, rambunctious, brutish kid so willing and able to push me to the absolute limit of my tolerance was a budding young man of character, principle, loyalty to his peers, and respect for everyone.

Band of Brothers

Before the Injury

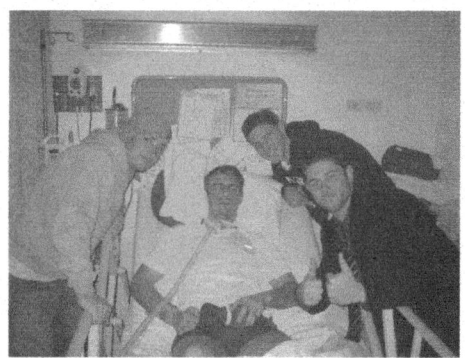

While in a coma

Finally Home

CHAPTER 10

COMPLICATIONS OF A BROKEN BRAIN

"Courage Dear Heart."

—C.S. Lewis

There are times in our lives when we face a substantial change in the kind of lifestyle we are obliged to lead, owing to some kind of significant transition, whether that transition is a major accomplishment achieved, or quite to the contrary, something we never would have anticipated or wanted. For example, the college graduate transitions from a world of textbooks and classrooms to the competitive world of business or industry. Or the happily wedded couple returns home from the honeymoon only to face the unfamiliar, shared challenges of married life, and then there is the spouse who loses a partner and must forge a new course alone. Yet it is difficult to imagine a transformative life change more profoundly dramatic and more pervasive than that which inevitably occurred to our entire family's routine way of life. Extending even further to our relatives, friends, and business associates for when Preston was finally able to come home after his traumatic injury.

We were naturally both relieved and ecstatic to be bringing our son home with us, finally, but we could only imagine what would be entailed in taking care of him essentially all by ourselves. After all, Preston could not walk or talk, and with his thought processing being extremely slow, communication with him was very difficult, so he required tending to his every need 24/7. We set him up in a hospital style adjustable bed in the middle of our family room on the first floor, in part for convenience in taking care of him, in part because we had no means of getting him upstairs to his bedroom. So, we hired a contractor to convert a downstairs bathroom to make it fully handicapped accessible with a walk-in shower, handrails and other essential fixtures. Just standing erect was extremely difficult for Preston, as he would get extremely ill after just a few minutes of being on his feet; after seven months of being mostly confined to hospital beds his body was simply not used to prolonged standing, to the point where it would actually cause him to become dizzy and make him throw up. At Children's Hospital the therapists used a heads-up tilt table, on which Preston would lay flat on his back, strapped on with his feet resting on a footplate, which then would be tilted upward anywhere between 60 to 80 degrees to mechanically place him on his feet. The procedure was very important in order to get Preston's body to adjust to a standing position after months of being confined in bed.

Unfortunately, this procedure would typically make him dreadfully sick due to an elevated heart rate and low blood pressure. He was never able to complete the 20-minute session and subsequently was diagnosed with orthostatic hypotension. When the body moves to a standing position, the cardiovascular system senses this movement and must adjust in order to prevent gravity from causing too much blood to rush towards the legs triggering an excessive drop in blood pressure. The brain then does not get enough blood supply and begins to shut down, causing lightheadedness, confusion, nausea, and passing out.

Once he was home, several times a day, I would make Preston practice standing—just standing, never-mind actually walking—by leaning on the wall behind him while locking the wheels of his wheelchair in front of him, and onto which he could hold for balance, for as long as he could manage. However, it would not be long before his lips began turning a pale white and an ill expression of nausea on his face would indicate that he had had enough, usually within the space of only five or ten minutes at most.

Ted's daily routine continued pretty much as it had been before; out the door and off to work in the early morning, back home in the evening in time for dinner. The same could not be said for mine, however. Because I had my own thriving 24/7 business to run, and while I could accomplish some work from a remote computer setup at home, I had an outside office full of co-workers that I was obligated to manage on a regular basis just like any other business owner. The first at-home aides we hired to help with Preston's care while both Ted and I were out of the house were unable to drive him to his daily weekday Physical Therapy (PT) sessions.[4] That meant I would go to the office in the morning, return home about midday to take Preston to PT, go back to the office for a couple of hours, then return to the therapy facility to bring Preston back home, go back to the office for the rest of the afternoon, and finally go home at the end of the day to prepare dinner for my family. Evenings proved even harder for me personally as I was now sleeping downstairs on the couch due to the bright light and email alerts from my computer that keep Ted wake and me working throughout the night. I was managing only a couple hours of sleep a day. It was difficult, exhausting, and honestly, a source of relentless anxiety, fear, and even depression, for which I am not ashamed to admit that I would eventually seek the professional help of a psychologist. Burning the candle at both ends as a 24/7 business owner and a 24/7 caregiver for years did not burn more light, it eventually led to a burn out and prove evident that it was time for a life evaluation.

And yet through it all, Preston slowly improved. After about nine months of caring for him at home, we started to see his old familiar, gregarious personality coming back; his devilish sense of humor appeared to be returning, the twinkle in his eyes rekindled. His physical therapy workouts were becoming stronger and more rigorous, a fact that was actually documented on video in the ESPN report, which briefly shows Preston looking strong while going through his paces on a step-machine. All positive signs and incremental improvements that gave Ted and me tremendous hope.

---

4   Home-aides are generally hesitant to drive their patients due to possible accident liabilities and wear and tear on their personal cars, so they often will not mention that they can offer this service. Years after Preston's injury when I finally inquired to our home care agency about providing transportation, they indicated that our home-aide would happily drive Preston to appointments and back if we were willing to provide the vehicle. This was enormously helpful to me, and I only wish the aide had be more forthcoming and told us sooner!

But then all the sudden it happens….a curve ball. Every batter can always expect to be thrown a curve ball; they just don't know when that will be. Just as we were all growing accustomed to Preston's adversities and effectively confronting them head on, a dirty curve ball was cast. Because the next challenging problem Preston had to tackle, and a new twist in his recovery, was seizures. We had been doing everything "right" for him, and it just did not seem fair that despite all of Preston's efforts to get his life back, he just couldn't seem to make it to home plate. My heart bled out for him and we all felt totally trounced, but we had to make a choice. We could allow ourselves to be destroyed, fall apart and just give up, or we could bounce back and hit that damn ball!

At first, I'd have to say that we really did not recognize the occurrence of these events. An epileptic seizure can manifest in the sufferer as nothing more than a kind of frozen, vacant stare lasting only 3 to 5 seconds or so. Given our son's massive cognitive and emotional deficits, attentional lapses of this sort probably seemed to us to be yet another marker of the brain damage he had suffered. Absence seizures, as they are called, can be extremely deceptive because to the outside observer they may look precisely like someone simply collecting their thoughts. In point of fact, however, the doctors had warned us that the scarring of Preston's brain tissue as a result of his massive injury could very likely lead to the occurrence of such seizures, which in many cases, they indicated, begin about two years after the injury. And ironically, I remember a time nearly three years out that Ted and I optimistically speculated that Preston appeared to have somehow dodged that bullet. We couldn't have been more wrong.

Because over time, Preston's seizures progressively worsened in intensity, variety, and frequency. In addition to the absence seizures, Preston began to suffer with more serious Myoclonic and Grand Mal seizures, the latter primarily in the middle of the night interrupting his sleep. At first, I thought that Preston was just snoring, but I quickly realized by the uncharacteristic, jerky movements of his body that he was actually seizing. Grand Mal seizures are believed to be caused by abnormal electrical activity throughout the brain. Myoclonic seizures are generally brief, shock-like jerking or twitching of a muscle or a group of muscles lasting only a second or two; however, in severe cases they can often happen multiple times in rapid succession lasting up to 30 minutes. Preston's Grand Mal seizures would cause loss of consciousness, foaming at the mouth, and violent muscle contractions, the kind of event that most people associate with the sufferer falling to the ground and going into dangerous convulsions. We always had an emergency rescue treatment kit of Dilantin right next to his bed to provide a way to stop the seizure activity and prevent an emergency situation if the seizure were to continue too long. This treatment was frightening in and of itself, in part because when it was needed, it had to be administered slowly or risk severe cardiovascular complications. If that weren't enough, Preston also began suffering what are alternatively called Partial Complex, or Focal Impaired Awareness seizures. Common in people with epilepsy and also known to occur in people with Cerebral Palsy, Partial Complex seizures also precipitate uncontrolled movement of limbs and other body parts, and in Preston's case it appeared that his body always pulled to the right when he suffered one of these events. By the summer of 2009, three years after he came home from Children's Hospital, Preston was experiencing between 10 and 20 seizures a day, and they were only getting worse.

In light of this deeply disturbing concern, we consulted back with Dr. Saadi Ghatan, a leading New York neurosurgeon, currently the Chair of Neurosurgery at Mount Sinai West and Director of the Pediatric Neurosurgery Program of the Mount Sinai Health System, and the doctor who had performed the surgery to attach Preston's prosthetic skull. Since the anti-seizure medications Preston was taking at the time were not controlling his seizures, Dr. Ghatan recommended as a means of treatment to relieve my son's chronic seizures was nothing short of terrifying. He recommended a surgical procedure in which he would disconnect the right frontal lobe from the rest of Preston's brain. As the region most damaged in the on-field collision at Duquesne and consequently where most of the subsequent scarring of brain tissue had occurred, Dr. Ghatan believed that it was from within the right frontal lobe that the seizures were originating, based on his preliminary tests.

At first, along with Ted and Preston, I was all in for doing this radical surgery, primarily because Dr. Ghatan assured us all that the surgery was the best solution for Preston. However, right before the surgery I became scared. Very scared.

I reasoned that medical science is coming up with new, more effective drugs and drug therapies all the time, and I tried to hold fast to the belief that one day very soon they would develop a medication that would be successful in relieving Preston's seizures. Moreover, to me, surgery that would effectively sever even more neurological connections with the brain seemed a lot like doing even more damage; after all, once the disconnect was performed, there would be no going back. I fought against this procedure as bravely as I could bring myself to be, yet both Preston and Ted were resolute in support of it. Preston in particular was most adamant about it; he desperately wanted relief once and for all from the incessant seizures. I could fully understand and feel his anguish over this, as well as his determination to put an end to these painful events. In reality given his circumstances, it would prove impossible for me to oppose my boy's fervent wishes in this regard. Who could? Also of great concern, Dr. Ghatan and his colleague, neurologist Dr. Steven Wolff, explained that if allowed to continue unabated, Preston's seizures would very likely cause further damage to his brain and as a result his condition would start to regress. Time, it seemed, was of the essence, and it was not on our side. And so the decision was made.

About six days prior to the planned disconnect surgery, Drs. Ghatan and Wolff removed the prosthetic skull from the right side of Preston's head and began the painstaking and critically dangerous task of scrapping away the scar tissue that had developed on the surface of Preston's brain. This operation would take an excruciating eight hours—two hours longer than the frontal lobe disconnect would take a week later—and once that was completed, the doctors placed an electrode grid on the brain that they would video-monitor to try to identify the precise locations from which the seizures were coming. This diagnostic procedure is called brain mapping or focus mapping. Finally, the doctors drilled a hole in the top of Preston's head through which they ran the wires that were connected to the implanted electrode grid before replacing the prosthetic to close up Preston's skull. The whole procedure was about as harrowing an ordeal as anyone could imagine, yet there was more medically inflicted horror to come.

Epileptic seizures don't happen on queue of course, so in order to efficiently monitor Preston's seizures, the medical team needed to deliberately induce them, and they would do this for the next five days leading up to the disconnect surgery.

They needed to induce seizures!

For me those five agonizing days may have been the most terrifying days of my son's whole saga to-date, in fact they may have been the most terrifying days of my entire life: Imagine the colossal irony of having to create, on purpose, the very phenomena that you are trying to prevent from happening on its own accord. During this period Preston experienced innumerable, massive Grand Mal seizures while several doctors stood at the ready to inject Dilantin to stop them if they exceeded five minutes, after which they could do very serious damage. It would take Preston an hour or more to come out of the fog after these major seizures, and when he finally did he was as exhausted as if he had just run a marathon. Meanwhile he suffered with constant, throbbing headaches and an incessant high fever that made him sweat profusely and constantly no matter how cold the nursing staff turned down the temperature in his room. He also had persistent nausea that made it difficult for him to keep food down, if he was even able to eat anything in the first place. In the end, the video monitoring confirmed Dr. Ghatan's suspicion that most of Preston's seizures were originating in the right frontal lobe of his brain.

It goes without saying that I did a lot of praying during that week and somehow managed to suppress my terrified tears so as not to worry Preston. However, on the day of the operation I was standing alone just outside Preston's room, watching as he was being prepped for his early morning surgery. This was it, there would be no going back. My worry had reached its pinnacle and I could no longer hold back my tears, and I began quietly weeping. That's when, quite uncharacteristically I think, Dr. Ghatan came over and gave me a hug. Then with his hands firmly on my shoulders, he looked me directly in the eyes and quite convincingly said, "You are doing the right thing." All I could do was nod and hope, and on July 31 of 2009 at St. Luke's Roosevelt Hospital in New York, Dr. Ghatan performed a six-hour, irreversible, right frontal lobe disconnect on Preston.

Throughout this ordeal there had been many hours—in fact too many hours—that Ted and I sat in cold unassuming waiting rooms with the anticipation of receiving some sort of news on Preston—good or bad. The wait, as you can imagine, is always filled with intense anxiety, enormous stress, and of course, abject fear of the outcome. The worst part of the wait is always the unoccupied time, the silence, just sitting and waiting; waiting for any updates. During this wait, as usual, my stomach ached and my heart was racing without pause.

"What is taking so long?" I restlessly demanded. "That damn clock on the wall is beginning to annoy me," I commented to Ted. "I think it's not working right, it is moving too slow!"

But Ted, with his characteristic, inattentive mindset, gave no reaction to my admittedly senseless observation. I guess there are times when it is best to just respect the silence, and to use it to reflect, and of course; to pray. A tranquil moment to sit in the stillness and allow the Word of God to whisper, *courage, dear heart.*

And then it was finally over! Another life-altering, incredibly complicated surgery was finally over and done. And while I was tremendously relieved, I was also very mindful of the fact that there would be no turning back forever!

When Preston came out of the operating room, much to my anguish and motherly heartbreak, my boy was in enormous pain; he was running a fever of 101.7 degrees, his face was so frighteningly swollen, to the point that he could not open his right eye, and there was no movement in his left arm, though he could manage to move his other limbs slightly. His unseen brain, re-traumatized by the shock of this latest surgical intrusion we were told, was also swollen as a result, but this was normal and the swelling would subside over time. But then, just three days later, he developed pneumonia and had to be put on a ventilator to do his breathing for him. He had also become so physically weak that the nurses were instructed to snake a feeding tube through his nose and into his stomach to provide critically needed nourishment in an effort to try to build up his strength. Witnessing my son's continued suffering and the trauma of the possibility of losing him all over again was agonizing. Standing at his bedside as I tenderly caressed his motionless arm, I leaned over and softly whispered into his ear; "Courage dear heart."

Describing the operation as quite successful, Dr. Ghatan would later tell us that the right frontal lobe was so damaged that he believed Preston was no longer using it, and the only reason he decided not to remove it entirely was because it was needed to ensure adequate blood flow. Since this surgery, Preston has not suffered any more seizures. Regardless, however, this major surgery brought Preston back to square one and once again he was unable to walk or talk; despite Dr. Ghatan's profuse assurances that our son, after a suitable recovery period of perhaps several months, would be physically and cognitively as good in terms of his rehabilitative progress after the disconnect surgery as he was before it. This would turn out not to be the case at all. Despite the doctor's assurance that Preston would not regress as a consequence of the disconnect surgery, he did in fact regress significantly to a point that might have even been lower, at least for a brief time, than where he was right after the SIS injury itself. At one point shortly afterward, Ted was sitting at Preston's bedside when he noticed that he was crying.

"What's wrong?" Ted asked.

"Nothing works," Preston tearfully managed to mouth out. It was so heartbreaking to feel his helplessness.

* * * * *

"Our stars are not where we last admired them. Our homes crumble and we don't know which place to long for."

—Ann Druyan

Traumatic, catastrophic events inevitably transform not only the victim of the event but also those around who love and care about the victim. Over the long seven months of hospitalizations from the ICU at Mercy Hospital in Pittsburgh to the rehab facility at Children's Hospital, and now, here again for a solid month at St. Luke's Roosevelt, every day and night either Ted or I, or both of us, had kept a virtually uninterrupted vigil by Preston's bedside. This of course would leave our Perry feeling abandoned, confused and distraught once again, in uncomfortable situations where he was often left under the care of others, if not simply left to himself. I have to confess that there were moments when I personally was incapable of even thinking about him during these days and months, as I could not face his heartache of knowing how much he was suffering, too. It was all so overwhelming, and the reality was I was grieving. We were all grieving, just in different ways. It was as though it was impossible for me to grieve in sufficient quantity for both of my sons and what each of them was going through, and because Preston's physical, cognitive, and emotional trauma was so much more obvious, I tended to focus all of my attention on him and failed to recognize Perry's deep yet unspoken psychological and emotional distress. And as I became so preoccupied with the fear that I could lose Preston entirely, I did not see or realize that in another way I was slowly losing my precious young son, my Perry.

So many time's we adults think that kids are too immature to comprehend the pain of a loss and expect them to just get over it and move on because they are young, they are resilient. Perry was only 17 years old and a senior in high school when Preston was injured; so very impressionable and just starting to find his way in life. The two of them had plans to play football at La Salle, finally to play together on the same team after Perry graduated high school. Preston had always watched out for him, he was Perry's strength and guiding force. Now that strength and guidance were gone, and I imagined that Perry must have felt like someone without a warm coat on a cold day. He must have felt naked and alone and in need of finding a way to feel warm and protected once again. But he did not know how. He needed hugs and reassurance and I gave him the absence of comfort and the fear of the unknown. At his tender age Perry was not capable of simply getting over this, nor should I have expected him to; I realize that now. He needed to grow through this with the love and support of his family. Where were we? Always at the hospital; every day, every moment, and not realizing that an emotional injury was progressively building within Perry, and the psychological scars that would remain would be every bit as damaging as the physical scars on Preston's brain tissue that had pitched him into the throes of violent epileptic seizures.

After we had initially brought Preston home from Pittsburgh, I could not understand why Perry so often refused to come to the hospital to visit his stricken brother. And again, I confess that it disappointed and angered both Ted and me as much as it surprised and confused us. We tried to get Perry to come with us to visit, told him how much we missed him, and how much Preston wanted and needed to see him, but he would not come. This was perplexing. What was happening here?!

Perry was spending all of his time outside of school with his friends and their families. I could not help but wonder if perhaps Perry reached out to someone "out there" and became a victim of poor advice that may have influenced his off-putting demeanor towards us. Of course, I will never know if this was the case, but when you are grasping for straws in desperation, and as a mother, you feel that you must try to find some kind of answer for your child's hurtful actions, it's only human nature.

With his ambitious plans of joining his big brother as a student and football teammate at LaSalle in ruins, Perry twice attempted to attend college locally at highly respected Brookdale Community College, and twice failed out, though he certainly possessed the aptitude and the smarts to succeed. Although, it was obvious that his heart was never in it; he failed to go to his classes and lied about it, he was often out all night with his friends engaging in what I will only describe as self-destructive behavior (and leave it at that), and refusing to talk to either Ted or me when we tried unsuccessfully to confront him about it.

Yet in all fairness, even though Ted and I made absolutely sure that one of us was always with Preston at the hospital 24/7, the other was always at home in the evenings and weekends to spend time with Perry to try to tend to his needs as well. Still, it became apparent that Perry would try to avoid us by never coming home until the very late hours; sometimes three or four in the morning, or even towards dawn as the sun was coming up. When he did finally arrive home, he would never talk to us, but would walk straight past us, his cold glassy eyes never connecting with ours as he made his way up to his room and shut the door. I felt like he was punishing us at the cruelest level by withholding his love, knowing that it was hurting us. He did not understand that the person he was hurting the most was only himself by rejecting our love and avoiding any kind of relationship with us. While I tried not to let this affect me, it did. I knew he was hurting just like the rest of us, and I also knew that his pain, whether he would acknowledge it or deny it, demanded attention. He needed to come to terms with it and accept our love too.

Out of desperation, I admit I engaged in the foolish audacity to try to trick Perry into talking to my psychologist, implying that the conversation was intended to be on my behalf rather than his. He reluctantly agreed and while in the doctor's office he surmised rather quickly that he had been hoodwinked. Needless to say, this deceitful attempt to get Perry to talk backfired and he became infuriated with me. So, while my intention was only trying to help, any semblance of whatever relationship I had left with him at that point was basically annihilated.

I suppose, psychologically speaking, that it is impossible to definitively attribute Perry's troublesome and disturbing behavior during this difficult time directly to the tragedy of his big brother's injury, or even in part through his becoming disillusioned with the excruciating fact that it came by way of the very game that Perry loved every bit as much as did Preston. Or to speculate that it was nothing more than "normal" and inevitable teenage rebellion that he would have exhibited regardless of Preston's situation, though knowing the sweet person that Perry was and still is deep down inside, I find any such suggestion highly doubtful, even absurd. Still, I only know that Perry's behavior during what should have been his college years after Preston's accident became more aberrant and potentially self-destructive than it had ever been during his high school years before it, when he had seemed to be as well-adjusted and happy as any parent could expect their teenage son to be.

Fortunately however, one day out of the midst of my frustration regarding his stoic behavior and two failed attempts at the local college, I devised another plan to try to get through to Perry. My love for my youngest son is deep-seated, it's only unique unto him, irreplaceable, and will never waver and just like with Preston, I was not going to give up on him. That morning at breakfast, I handed my sullen teenager a piece of paper and a pen and I instructed him to write down the five things that he most loved to do.

Predictably of course, Perry moaned and complained about what a stupid, absurd, ridiculous (and on and on), not to mention onerous, exercise I was tasking him with.

"Whatever," I said, and I instructed him, "Just humor me and do it." And with that I left for the office. When I returned home in the early evening I was pleasantly surprised to see that Perry had actually scribbled down five things on the paper and left it in the middle of the kitchen table. Eagerly I grabbed this paper with the hope that I could finally get some answers to help Perry figure out and find his path. At the top of the list, Perry's #1 was "Music," followed by "Movies" as #2. Number three was football, which I immediately discounted because, well, I think I can be forgiven for being relieved by the knowledge that unlike the endowed godlike physique of his older brother, Perry thankfully did not possess the physical attributes required to make a sustainable career as a player in the NFL. In addition and more importantly, after Preston's life-changing injury from football, this game was now outlawed in our house.

Fourth on the list, was playing guitar. Perry is an excellent self-taught guitar player, and as I think about it now, there is something very telling about that "self-taught" part. Love for the instrument or not, Perry would never have sat still for lessons from a teacher-professional; that just isn't his way. However, it is almost impossible to forget his last Item #5. Perry wrote that he loved "dogs." Why?? Because, "Dogs don't ask you to write out stupid lists." Now, that is my Perry, through and through.

In any event, when I sat down with Perry to talk about his list, I pointed to his #1 and #2 entries of music and movies, and I suggested that perhaps he would be interested in attending a film school and work towards a career in the movie or television entertainment industry.

"You mean I can do that?" he asked enthusiastically. I said, "Of course, if that is what you will make you happy."

The long and the short of it was that within one week after he wrote the list, the two us flew to Florida to talk to the administrators of an accredited film school, and shortly thereafter, Perry happily left for Full Sail University in Winter Park, Florida, less than 25 miles from Disneyworld. Full Sail is a rather unique university offering academic degree programs primarily focused on audio, film, and media production, as well as video game design and animation, and more recently offering studies in augmented and virtual reality production related to the media and entertainment industries. There Perry earned his Bachelor of Science degree in Film based on a very aggressive 2-year degree program. Once he had achieved that, I suggested that he continue at Full Sail to earn a business degree also, pointing out that it would be as just as important for him to learn the *business* of making films or TV programs as it was to have learned the technical sciences of movie production. To my delight Perry agreed; however, midway through his studies, and only a few credits shy of earning a business degree, he decided he was done with school and abruptly returned home.

While I was disappointed that my son once again did not follow through and finish what he had started, I felt on the one hand that he had at least gotten some of the business knowledge if not the paper. And on the other, I felt that just perhaps, I may have had made some small inroad toward reconnecting with Perry, through all the hurt and distance that had come between us. One thing was clear, I believe: Perry really needed that time to go out on his own and forge his own journey forward.

Perry and our dog Rex

For Preston after his disconnect surgery, it did indeed seem that nothing worked. Over most of the entire month of August following the surgery, he struggled just to try to be passably comfortable in his ICU bed—he seemed to struggle just to survive—with the ever-present feeding tube down his throat, a catheter in his groin, an IV in his arm, and the wires from numerous diagnostic monitors attached to his head and chest. At times the nurses were compelled to tie his arms to the handrails to prevent him from trying to rip out the feeding tube or more importantly the breathing tube! He constantly veered in and out of high fever, and the first several days after the surgery, as I pointed out earlier, Preston was also on a ventilator lying completely conscious while this medical device provided oxygen through the breathing tube. This process of intubation is inserting a breathing tube that passes through the mouth and into the airway keeping air flowing into the lungs. If that wasn't enough, suctioning to remove his secretions by the use of a catheter had to be performed to clean the tube. This was scary and very intimidating, I felt like I was adding to his pain and discomfort, but it had to be done. The agony from this breathing tube as well as other probes made it difficult for Preston of course. But having to witness his agonized body language displaying his suffering was an awful and traumatic experience for all of us. Most patients who are placed on a ventilator, may God bless them, are in pretty rough shape and consequently unconscious, so they are totally unaware of being on the device and thus don't feel it. But Preston was quite awake and did; it was impossible for him to even try to ignore the fact, like when someone tells you not to think about pink elephants, only much worse than that.

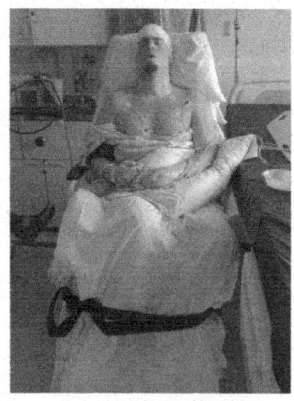
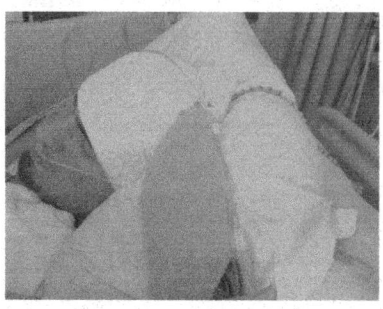
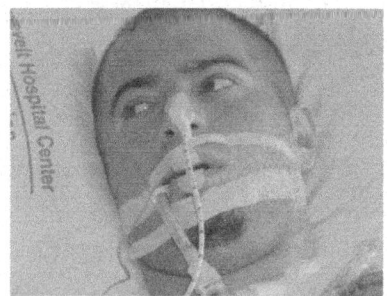
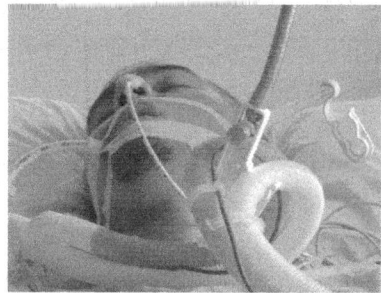

Awake with tubes going down his nose and throat.

I had started writing a journal about ten days before the disconnect surgery was slated to take place. I recognized that this was going to be another ordeal of a lifetime for Preston and our family, and I wanted to write about it, if for no other reason, just to be able to one day tell him about his courageous and undaunted fight for his life. Patients with brain injuries like Preston's often experience post-traumatic amnesia; a loss of memory, often right from the moment of the original TBI. In such cases, the patient does not remember the pain they endured, their struggles, the medical procedures and/or surgeries they underwent, or even why they are in the hospital at all. I would like to believe that not remembering all the painful horrors he had endured on his road to recovery was a small blessing. But I still believed a permanent record of his valor ought to be made in writing.

So, I had learned that there was a website where you can journal the progress of your loved one as a means of actively keeping family and friends updated during these difficult times of surgery and recovery. CaringBridge. org uses an online medical journal format in which you create your own personal website through which they provide you with the tools to post progress updates and pictures. The site also gives folks on the outside, friends, family, and others, the ability to respond directly to each update with words of love and support. The invaluable messages of encouragement, love and strength we received gave us hope and reassurance that we were not alone during this highly stressful period.

In addition, later when your loved one returns home from the hospital, if you wish, you may have your journal printed in a nice hardcover book to refer to in the future. In any case, my journal entries reveal numerous instances in which Preston's once Adonis-like body failed to operate properly in terms of the most routine of tasks. For just one example, for a day or two, Preston literally could not stick out his tongue, and when he finally could manage that, for another day or so he could not draw it back in without assistance. His body was like some sort of electronic robot that had short circuits all over the place, and in fact, the neurosurgeons explained that it would take time—as long as six months—for his brain to make new synaptic connections to essentially "rewire" the ones that had been severed surgically. But I knew my boy's determination, and I knew he would fight his way back much faster than that. At least I hoped he would!

Preston was also plagued with unrelenting hiccups again, which according to the nurses may have been a side effect of the corticosteroids needed to dampen his body's immune response and reduce swelling after the operation. I wrote in my journal, "Can you imagine having the worst headache of your life and you [also] have the hiccups?!!!" But as I reflect on that now, I might have easily have asked if one could imagine having a plague of hiccups while at the same time having a feeding tube down your throat! Plus being on a ventilator! By the time the feeding tube was finally removed—which is to say, by the time Preston finally succeeded in ripping it out right through his nose about two weeks after the surgery—the nurses decided against reinserting it because at that point on top of everything else, Preston also had probably the worst sore throat of his entire life!

In addition to playing an important role in cognitive skills like problem solving, memory, language, and judgement, the frontal lobes of the brain are also considered to be our emotional control center and the seat of our personality. Accordingly, one of the most common effects of frontal lobe damage can be significant changes or swings in mood or temperament. In Preston's case, in addition to the severing of vital neuro-synaptic connections, the disconnect surgery had also very likely created chemical imbalances, specifically affecting the regular flow of neurotransmitters. While we by all means wanted to see Preston's always ebullient personality start to return during this ambiguous time, I had an uneasy feeling that something was dreadfully wrong. Because for a time, Preston was absent of any body language, displayed vacant facial expressions revealing a terrifying sense of emptiness; a desolation, as if he were just a being of existence, but not of any mental substance. Aristotle put it like this: "The energy of the mind is the essence of life."

Was there no end to the collateral discomfiture and pain my boy must endure?

And to be perfectly honest about it, from time to time I could not look at all these cascading events threatening my boy's life day after day without reflecting that all of this ongoing and seemingly endless ordeal was a result of playing football!

From the extensive research I had done, and despite Dr. Ghatan's auspicious yet unrealized predictions for Preston's anticipated state of wellbeing after the surgery, I do not believe that Ted or I truly grasped the real potential for regression after such a radical procedure. While the surgery would indeed prove extremely successful in relieving Preston's seizures, and while we were very grateful to Drs. Ghatan and Wolfe for that, unfortunately there would be damaging consequences as well. As mentioned previously, the frontal lobes of the brain control many functions relating to motivation, attention, and concentration, to name just a few. Disconnecting this part of the brain causes significant changes to these functions that Preston would ultimately exhibit. So for me personally, I cannot say that the surgery was a total success with respect to what we anticipated. I guess William Osler said it best; "Medicine is a science of uncertainty and an art of probability." Yet despite it all, from the moment Preston's disconnect surgery had been successfully completed, Ted and I were determined and singularly focused on getting him up and active and working his various speech, cognitive, and physical therapies.

That first week after, as I noted, all Preston wanted to do, and in fact to be fair, all that it seemed he could do, was sleep, which was probably a Godsend given how much pain and discomfort he was in whenever he was awake. Yet even the nurses acknowledged that he needed to be more alert, although they said this paradoxically as they were pumping him with morphine to try to ward off the pain.

A major milestone occurred on August 7th when Preston was taken off the ventilator and began to be phased out of the ICU in a gradual step-down process that was completed by the 15th of the month. During this time another great sign—for what it's worth—Preston began shamelessly flirting with the nurses! As mentioned previously, when Preston pulled out his feeding tube, it was actually a good thing. He had lost 30 pounds in three weeks (I joked to my women friends in my journal that only men could lose weight that swiftly!), he was not taking well to the liquid food he had been getting through the tube, and we needed to get him eating solid food on his own.

We also knew from previous experience that we could not let Preston lie around in his bed languishing; we needed to get him up and moving and exercising; to get both body and brain working again, and now after the disconnect surgery, to get both working *together* again. It sometimes felt as though all the work that was done and all of the progress that had been made over the previous four years was now in vain and we had to start all over again. We all knew that starting all over and rebuilding Preston's life again was going to require a tremendous amount of inner strength, courage, faith, and confidence from all of us. I knew we were fully up to the task, but was Preston up to it, after this radical, life-changing surgery?

At this point I could go into a great deal of detail about Preston's slow but steady progress in Roosevelt Hospital, from first managing to sit on his own on the edge of his bed for 20 minutes or so, to standing on his own and taking his first steps. And while I know that the PT folks at Roosevelt did what they could to help, their 10- to 15-minute therapy sessions simply were not adequate, and whenever Preston was awake, I was constantly exercising his arms and legs and neck. I can tell you that there were many complications along the way, but what Preston really needed now was to get out of the hospital and be transferred to a rehabilitation facility where he could really get down to work with in a serious regimen of PT; only there would he make a more rapid, efficient, and effective recovery. And so, Ted and I constantly pushed and challenged Preston, once again never leaving his side. At one point after Preston had pulled out the feeding tube, and concerned about his weight loss, the nurses had contemplated putting a feeding tube or peg directly into his stomach. But fortunately when they came to do the procedure, Ted was there to stop them, stating flatly, "Oh no, absolutely not. He is eating and we do not want a peg." And it was true, because earlier that same day, ironically enough, Preston had enjoyed his very first Wendy's Frosty, one of his favorites.

All I can say is that all of that hard work and persistence finally paid off: Preston was moved to the Health South Rehabilitation Hospital in Tinton Falls, New Jersey on August 18th. Then, after 22 days of intensive, determined, and enormously hard work, Preston came home again on September 9th, 2009, we hoped this time for good.

CHAPTER 11

THE VIEW AFTER THE CLIMB

*"The flower that blooms in adversity
is the rarest and most beautiful of all."*

—Walt Disney

From the moment Preston first came home from Children's Specialized Hospital, there never was a time—nor will there ever be, I would add—when we gave up on finding a new therapy or treatment that might help him to improve, and hopefully to get Preston to where he could live some sort of an independent life again. I began furiously researching all of the conventional scientific medical literature for answers, but I also investigated emerging non-conventional treatment approaches as well. When it became apparent that the then-available conventional means might not be sufficient or might not yield satisfactory results, we sought out the non-conventional techniques that seemed to have some scientific medical merit, or which seemed to have achieved some positive results with other patients whose plights were similar to Preston's. Modern medicine is always changing, I have always reasoned; meaning that new things are discovered and advances in treatments are made every day. That belief had formed the fundamental basis for my objection to Preston's brain disconnect surgery. In the early 2000's perhaps the most promising area of research was that of stem cell therapy, the use of which was targeted to treating degenerative brain diseases like Parkinson's and Alzheimer's as well as brain and spinal cord injuries resulting from traumatic injury or stroke. Preston seemed the perfect candidate.

Because it was still in its infancy, stem cell treatment was not approved in the U.S., so in October of 2007 we traveled to a clinic in Germany, in the city of Cologne. There the doctors collected 30 vials of bone marrow from Preston's right hip from which they subsequently were able to extract 11 million stem cells. One million of those stem cells were then injected into Preston's thighs while the other 10 million were re-implanted into his cerebro-spinal fluid through a lumbar puncture. I have to say that we were made very hopeful after that first stem cell treatment because we seemed to see some improvement, particularly with the slow but steady return of Preston's speech and person-ality. Unfortunately, as I described in the preceding chapter, less than a year later Preston was experiencing seizures that were increasing in both number and severity, a development that was clearly impeding his progress, and which of course became the primary issue of deepest concern, ultimately leading to his frontal lobe disconnect surgery.

Nevertheless, the very promising improvement we believed we saw in our son as a result of that first stem cell treatment buoyed us with sufficient optimism and confidence to attempt three more procedures that were per-formed in the years after his disconnect surgery, one in Dusseldorf, Germany in October of 2010, the other two in Mexico in later years. Each of these sub-sequent procedures was informed and modified in accordance with newly unfolding research in stem cell technology emanating from the growing body of experimental clinical research data, as more and more stem cell treatments were given to patients around the world.

For example, the doctors in Germany explained that one potential drawback of re-implanting the stem cells into the spine (via lumbar puncture) was that from there, the cells could travel anywhere in the body. There was no way of knowing where the cells would actually go, nor certainly any way for the doctors to direct those cells to the area of the body that most needed them. So for the second procedure in Dusseldorf, the five million stem cells that were extracted from Preston's bone marrow for that procedure were re-implanted directly into his brain in the hope that they would localize within the cranium and do their good work there. In similar fashion, the subsequent stem cell treatments done in Mexico both specifically employed the use of stem cells isolated from donated placenta which would offer certain vital, highly adaptive advantages due to their embryonic origin.

The important point is that all of Preston's stem cell treatments were clinically different designs and each built upon the latest emerging stem cell research findings that were compelling enough to convince us they were worth trying with Preston. Simply put, we did not subject Preston to the same exact procedure over and over again. Yet regardless, and quite sadly, we saw no appreciable improvement in our son's condition after the treatments in Dusseldorf and Mexico. Furthermore, I must acknowledge in hindsight that today, 12 years after the first stem cell treatment in late 2007, it remains inconclusive at best as to whether the gradual improvement that we thought we observed in Preston after that procedure was in fact due directly to the stem cell therapy, or was instead attributable to wishful thinking in the extreme on our part, or if it was even simply a manifestation of the normal healing process quite independent of the treatment altogether. It is perhaps worth noting here that as of this writing in 2019, stem cell therapy in the U.S. remains highly restricted by the FDA.

Of course, stem cell therapy has only been one of many treatments we have attempted. For another example, we twice took Preston to a clinic in Florida where he received peri-spinal etanercept treatments. You might know that etanercept is the FDA approved biopharmaceutical agent marketed as the prescription drug Embrel® and used to treat rheumatoid arthritis, juvenile idiopathic arthritis and psoriatic arthritis, plaque psoriasis, and a serious form of spinal arthritis. However, etanercept has also been used experimentally to try to reduce the persistent or long-term neuroinflammatory response that often follows serious brain injury due to stroke or TBI. In other words, treatment with etanercept may help reduce inflammation and restore proper functioning of brain tissue and the central nervous system. Some studies have shown "statistically significant improvements in motor impairment, spasticity, sensory impairment, cognition, psychological/behavioral function, aphasia and pain" (Tobinick et. al., 2012) through the application of peri-spinal etanercept treatment. Unfortunately, while such study results made us extremely hopeful, we did not notice any encouraging response to this treatment either.

The list goes on and on: From August of 2010 through June of 2011, Preston received over 100 Hyperbaric Oxygenation Therapy (HBOT) treatments administered twice weekly at a therapy center in Parsippany. The only reason we had to cease these treatments was because 100 "dives" is the medically advised limit, although in point of fact we saw little improvement as a result of these treatments. In addition, we administered Methyl-B12 shots every morning in Preston's buttocks for almost four years. Mainly used with children with autism, Methyl B12 is thought to unlock the areas of the brain that control and support verbalization and effective communication skills. Here again, however we saw no major improvements for Preston, and all he seemed to get from these treatments were the unsightly B-12 tattoo markings all over his tail end.

As recently as 2018, Preston, Ted, and I spent three weeks in Texas where Preston received treatment from a highly innovative, experimental research clinic that worked primarily with trying to improve his balance, based on a theory the doctors there had developed with respect to the importance of vision in patients with brain injury issues. Impaired balance, difficult walking and no peripheral vision in his left eye in particular, are all things that Preston struggles with every single day. Because of these issues even to the present day, Preston has developed tremendous fear which we believe is the main reason why he falls at times when walking on his own. Quite unfortunately, despite some promising indications in Preston during that very brief span of time, the Texas clinic closed down shortly thereafter.

However, determined to never surrender to this devastating injury, through my continuing research I came across another similar clinic in Colorado that Preston attended in the fall of 2019. In addition to their research-based diagnostics to evaluate Preston's functioning in specific areas of the brain, he received a Regenerative Cell treatment injection of stem cells followed by exosomes that was administered through the nose. Similar to the treatments Preston received in Mexico, these cells for the Regenerative Cell

Treatment are collected from mothers who have donated their placental tissue--specifically, from the Wharton's Jelly layer of the umbilical cord. Wharton's jelly is a gelatinous substance in the umbilical cord that consists of a network of structural biomolecules, pericytes, mesenchymal stem cells, cytokines, chemokines, and growth factors. The mesenchymal stem cells are multipotent stem cells that can differentiate into a number of other cell types including Neurons (brain cells), making it theoretically possible to repair the damaged areas of the brain, restore function, and prevent further neurodegeneration. The exosomes act as sort of a fertilizer helping these cells to communicate with the targeted cells. We are again hopeful that this treatment has developed over time and will offer a greater ability for cells to self-renew and increase the positive neurons.

One non-medical therapy suggested by Preston's PT was to take Preston Scuba diving (in a pool, of course). As mentioned earlier, Preston still struggles with swallowing food, especially when he tries to drink liquids. He also has difficulty with breathing, and exhaling in particular, which is most evident in his labored speech. When he tries to speak, he cannot gather the normal force of air behind his words, so he appears like someone trying to talk after running up several flights of stairs. In any case, Ted and I reasoned that the deliberate and more forceful breathing required to utilize Scuba gear in response to underwater pressure might help Preston to learn to breathe more powerfully out of the water, and to restore more normal function to esophagus, trachea and lungs. Not to mention that the "weightless" exercise associated with maneuvering underwater would hopefully be therapeutic for both body and brain.

Yet these are only a few of the more outside-the-box therapies we have tried and continue to try, in addition to the years of traditional therapies Preston has received. We will never tell Preston that there is nothing left to do. That would take away his hope. As our favorite family motto goes, as proclaimed by Mathesar, leader of the Thermians in the Star Trek spoof *Galaxy Quest*: *"Never give up….. never surrender!"* Perfectly said!

* * * * *

"Sometimes we must leave our true homes
for something greater to come."

—Mary-Jean Harris

The Sleeping Prophet Edgar Casey once said; "Each soul enters with a mission."

Throughout this book I have gone at considerable length to describe Preston's difficult journey resulting from a pair of concussions suffered roughly one month apart on separate football fields, and the numerous medical ordeals he has had to face along the way as a result. I have also explained the gruesome medical history, the various procedures we needed or decided to do to try to help our son recover some measure of his former self. Again I must reiterate, all from the game of football. Perhaps lost in all of this, it bears mention that we also tried to enable Preston to be as comfortable and happy as he could be under the circumstances, even as we pushed him hard when it came to rigorously doing his physical and cognitive therapies. Ted and I had decided; we resolved from very early on that there would be no sadness in our house, as it does nobody any good. We would allow only optimism and hope to pervade our home and lives. Given his substantial cognitive and physical limitations, trying to elevate the quality of Preston's life could be soul-crushingly difficult. Yet there came one moment when he communicated his paramount desire with unequivocal clarity—and it would turn out that we could actually do something quite tangible to help him fulfill that burning wish.

It happened that one afternoon while sitting with Preston in the kitchen just talking about things in general, that I casually asked him; "What do you miss most about the life you once had?"

Without any hesitation he softly said, "Girls."

We both timidly laughed. I suppose I shouldn't have been surprised, but I tried desperately to change the subject, although I really wasn't sure what I was looking for.

"Okay," I said, "Sure, I know, I realize that you are a young man, and it must be very hard for you but is there anything else you miss? Something that I may be able do something about?"

Again, without the slightest hesitation he motioned with his right hand as if he were in a car and said, "Driving."

I pondered his answer for a brief moment. "Driving, huh?" I said with some trepidation. "Hmmm. Well, Dad and I will have to think about that. You do understand that legally you are not allowed to drive due to your injury, right?"

Preston nodded; his steady gaze was solemn. It was clear that he really wanted this.

I could fully understand why Preston wanted to drive. There was just so little he could do on his own, and yet it was patently obvious that he longed for the kind of independence that most of us take for granted when we become of age, and in our lives there are precious few rites of passage that are more celebrated and cherished than achieving the privilege of driving. But even further, I surmised that he wanted to feel like a man again. He wanted to feel the wind blowing through his hair, to experience once again the thrill and excitement of being free, free from the bonds of his wheelchair, free from the endless days of just sitting and watching life outside that window, but instead being an active part of it. *WOW, how could we possibly tell him no?* I thought. There had to be a way to do this.

And when I thought about it, Perry was about to graduate from Full Sail University in Florida, and he was determined to find a place of his own, so it would be just the three of us remaining. Ted and I talked it over and thought that maybe we could get a house on a big piece of property—big enough with open fields, perhaps threaded with private trails or former farm lanes—where he could drive either a golf cart or a small ATV, since Preston would be prohibited from driving on public roads.

Furthermore, Ted was planning to retire within a year or so, and after a thorough life evaluation I had made the decision to retire early, sell my business and focus on Preston's care. After all, when it comes down to it, family is all what really truly matters. The more we talked the more we began to get excited about it for Preston. I will never forget the expression on his face when we told him that we had decided to move so he could drive and hopefully regain his confidence, a measure of independence, and, just perhaps, a motivation for him to recapture his life again. There have been only a few times in my life where my heart radiated with true, unbridled happiness for another human being. Witnessing that true splendor on his face was one of those exquisite times. So it was that in very short order, we were off to the Pocono Mountains area of Pennsylvania.

I suppose that leaving a home where you've lived for over two decades, and a community where the roots you put down ages ago extend very deep, is something that isn't easy for anyone with a heart. The memories of our home on Elisa Drive were created by the intricate details of its very own environment like a living, breathing entity with its own particular character and history; the unique yet fleeting history of our family. Ted and I had this home built from the ground up way back in the early 90's when our boys were both still very young. It was far more than just the furniture each room displayed or the warm carpets on which we sat and wrapped—and later excitedly unwrapped—our Christmas gifts each year.

Life never stood still in this house. Days were filled with work, football and baseball games and their subsequent social functions, parties on many weekends with friends or the boy's teammates, and summer barbecues and winter ski trips. Life was fun, exciting and good on Elisa Drive. After November 5th, 2005, much, if not all of that, had changed forever.

The truth was that after many years of trying to get Preston back on his feet and his life settled in, I found myself struggling with the imprints of the old Preston all over the house on Elisa Drive before his injury. I could see Preston coming in from the garage, with his beautiful contagious smile and his always upbeat persona shouting "I'm home!" as he would proceed to kick off his big shoes, sending them sailing across the room an into the corner where they would leave a new pair of ugly black marks on the wall.

"Oh come on, Preston!" I would holler at him. "Can't you be like a normal person and take your shoes off properly? Look what you are doing to the wall."

He would just grin that charming disarming grin and proceed to wrap his malodourous arms dripping with perspiration from practice around me for that dreadfully, grubby, sweaty hug. His way of course in getting the last word. Now, well over a decade hence, I would have given anything for him to kick off his shoes like that again, the wall be damned. Now these memories were only haunting me as I would watch him struggle just to maintain his balance coming in through the door.

His bedroom had once been filled with trophies plaques and medals, with dozens of photographs (mostly of sports), on the walls, and loud music blaring, full of the trajectory of his life during his time at Elisa Drive, in school, and on the athletic field, from football to track. But by now, all of that had been packed into boxes and put in storage and his room became essentially the empty shell of a young man whose hopes, dreams and plans for his future were severely and tragically diminished. I had remodeled his room three times throughout the 20 years, from the primary colors of a little boy to the black, teal, and silver geometric colors of space in his teens to the serene and muted aqua, green, and brown colors of an emerging adult. I can still picture him with his big feet dangling over the end of the twin bed he had completely outgrown, Preston begging for us to buy him a larger model. It was becoming all too hard to endure, all these memories. It has always been amazing to me how a house can seem like a living, breathing thing, even though it's dormant, but it's stays alive in our thoughts and in our memories and never leaves your mind.

And yet there is one heartbreaking, bitter memory that will forever burn in my psyche. When we had first brought Preston home from Children's Hospital, he was not yet able to walk. Consequently, we hired a contractor to build an access ramp to the side door to accommodate his wheelchair. But when the workers arrived and began installing it, Preston burst into tears and he began to panic, "No, I don't need it" he quietly exclaimed. That image of his extreme distress rips at my heart even to this day. Knowing my son's characteristic inner resolve and determination, I thought, and hoped at the time, that he simply did not believe—that he absolutely refused to believe—he was going to need that infernal ramp, at least not for very long. More horrifically however, I anguish over the thought that, at that moment, Preston may well have glimpsed the specter of grim finality, the potential permanence of his situation epitomized by the installation of that ramp, and it was just more than he could handle in his debilitated state. When I thought back on the bitter moment, I could readily acknowledge without equivocation that, yes, it was indeed time to move on, and leave behind these memories of the past.

I also feel, however, that it is important to emphasize here that we have never, ever, regarded Preston's situation as permanent; nor do I believe, has Preston himself, being the fighter that he is. In point of fact, throughout this entire ordeal, our family resolved never to dwell in sorrow or wallow in despair. We resolved instead to never give up. Through all of his football playing career and in spite of the poor teams with losing records he had played for; Preston had always played his heart out and never accepted defeat. This was absolutely no time to accept it!

In the scheme of things, however, Elisa Drive represented who we once were, our old identities and how we all changed through this tragedy, how we grew and hopefully became new and better versions of ourselves. The truth is, it is difficult to move forward when you are surrounded by everything that reminds you of who you used to be. We would certainly feel pangs of regret for making the decision to move, and perhaps even some guilt for feeling that we might not have fully appreciated our old life and our old, cherished home. But a house is just a house in the end. Moving away from Perry would be of course the hardest part, however respecting my own imperfections and limitations I have relinquished his heartache and his care into God's hands as I can humanly do no more. Leaving our many friends and so many of Preston friends was also going to be very difficult. I would come to gratefully and humbly acknowledge our past on Elisa Drive, honor it with cherished memories, and reflectively celebrate the good times we had there. But we had to make a choice, and we chose to move forward and take care of Preston and give him the life he deserved.

Then came the day when Preston finally got behind the wheel of the Gator ATV, both hands gripped tightly on the steering wheel, his attention focused on the road before him. Slowly his right foot begins to press the accelerator as this small mechanical vehicle of steel and plastic begins to move its way forward. Ted is in the Gator with Preston and I am standing off on the side of the driveway laden with a mixture of excitement, nervousness, and downright fear. Preston starts to smile as the Gator begins to pick up some speed, he feels the wind on his face as it flows through his hair and for the first time since his injury… he is in control. This was a truly amazing moment; that with all that his brain had endured he instinctively remembered how to drive! How wonderful it was to witness so much joy as his eyes lit up with the sheer excitement of the moment, his blissful smile radiated with such exultation that I knew we had made the right decision. Oh, my heart be happy, yet be calm, as I watch my beautiful boy drive down that long driveway gradually fading away among the nearby trees, with the wind softly nudging their branches arousing the leaves creating a whimsical sound of applause as he passes by. He is happy. He is free. He is king!

* * * * *

I have to confess that I never really understood the extent to which my boys risked serious injury, and even death when they were playing football, even in the Pop Warner days when the game seemed relatively harmless. Oh, there was never a big secret about the chance of sustaining a sprained ankle or wrist, or a broken arm or leg, and it was kind of a given that the kids would get some "manly" cuts and bruises. But the possibility of a severe life-changing injury or death? If I as a mother had known at the time the severe risks involved and the shocking statistics of deaths related to football, I think that Ted and I would have encouraged them to play a different sport that was not so violent and dangerous. Well, I know I personally would have.

Would my protests have changed anything? Possibly, but there are other forces in play as well, such as peer pressure and coaches seeking out the most athletically gifted kids and encouraging them to participate. As loving and caring parents we want our kids to be happy, to do the things they truly want to do, the things that interest and engage them, and ultimately to learn to make their own responsible decisions for themselves. I have to concede that by any measure of physical stature or athletic prowess, Preston's impressive 6'2" 225 lbs. body and his considerable competitive skills were tailor-made for football. What we tragically learned, of course, was that the brain inside his head was categorically *not* built for football. But then, one of the crucial lessons of this book is to understand that *no* human head is built for the kind of punishment in the form of repeated trauma from hits that players receive on the football field routinely—which is to say, day-in-and-day-out on both the practice field and in battle on game day.

Many years after his injury, addressing a large throng of people that had packed a concussion awareness event convened at a New Jersey hospital, Preston told the hushed crowd, "I could have sat out for one more game," to which the audience politely applauded. But later, speaking to a reporter, Preston expanded on that pronouncement, saying through the breath-starved bursts that still characterize his speech, "I could have... sat out... for a season.... But now... I will... sit out... for the rest... of my life."

* * * * *

Acceptance doesn't mean resignation; it means understanding that something is what it is and that there's got to be a way through it."

—Michael J. Fox

In late November of 2018, my son Perry now 30, married his longtime sweetheart Rachel. In his toast as best man to his younger brother and his bride, Preston told Perry that marrying Rachel was the smartest thing he ever did, and both Ted and I heartily agree. Since Preston could not speak very well, I decided to make a video of his speech complete with captions at the bottom and inserting music along with some home movies and pictures. Preston's speech was funny at times, as well as thoughtfully reminiscent in expressing his heartfelt love for his brother.

At the end of the speech something quite astonishing occurred. Clearly emotionally moved, Perry stood up and with tears in his eyes, he went over to his older brother and held him in an extended bear-hug so tightly, and that was when I knew: I knew at that pivotal moment Perry had just jumped a major hurdle to acceptance and compassion. The extreme emotion I felt for my two magnificent boys at that moment engulfed my entire being illuminating an aura of unmeasurable love all around me. It was a wonderful feeling, and a profoundly beautiful thing to witness, and there wasn't a dry eye in the room.

Today Perry's happiness radiates to all those around him and I hope that he has finally found some measure of peace. He and our lovely daughter-in-law live in New Jersey not far from the town of Marlboro where both our sons were raised. We live a couple of hours away from them, so we don't get to see them so often, much to my dismay. However, marriage is of course an adult stage of life for one's children, where you no longer expect them to "come home" quite so often anymore—where in fact if they do come home too often it may be a cause for concern!

While Perry has made great strides in his grieving I do not believe he has ever completely brought himself psychologically to fully, and deeply, process Preston's injury and the way it so drastically changed all of our lives forever. He does not see the daily caregiving that Preston requires. However, I believe that when he has a child of his own one day, he will come to fully understand and appreciate our day to day struggles as well as our parental imperfections during this period of catastrophic life-alterations. His reaction through withdrawal raises for me a kind of existential question that I don't really feel I have the complete answer to. Namely, how does one grieve for someone who is not dead?

Grief is mostly associated with death. After a loved one passes they are still forever in your heart, yet they are no longer in your physical life. This absence along with the normal expression of public mourning like a funeral allows for the grieving process to take place and in time you will be able to accept your loss. However, death is not the only cause of personal grief. "Consequential Grief" as I call it, is coming to terms in grieving the loss of the "old" person and embracing the "new" person who has suffered the consequence of a catastrophic life-altering event like Alzheimer's, as was my grandmother's condition, or a TBI as in Preston's life-altering case and which proved profoundly chaotic. We remember the "old" strong charismatic personality of Preston, only to now be forced to accept a "new" Preston that no longer has any resemblance to who he was. Although, I swear there are times when I look into his eyes I can see the old Preston trapped inside his physical prison. To witness the loss of his brawny abilities, the loss of his mental aptitude, and the loss of our family structure and lifestyle was overwhelming and a downright contradiction to everything we knew. To make matters worse and perhaps the hardest to bear, Preston was just 19 years old at the time of his TBI, so for me I also found myself grieving for the man he would have been, the husband, the father, the employee, the humanitarian, all the things that we all so often simply take for granted.

Accepting the reality of Preston's new life as well as our new world would not be easy if we really thought about it too much, so Ted and I made the decision to not dwell on or obsess about all of that. What I mean to say is that we knew there was never going to be any going back to the way things were, so we just embraced our newfound "mission," and moved forward. No sadness, remember. But then again, Preston makes it easy because he is such a beautiful loving soul. A soul that has been catastrophically humbled and who bravely tackles every single day with such tenacity, laughter, and love that it never ceases to amaze me. The paradox of this whole tragedy, is that I am both enormously distraught and yet immensely grateful at the same time, which is something truly astonishing to me that I cannot fully explain in words.

But one thing I have learned from this process is that everyone grieves at their own personal speed, and in ways that may or may not be understood or appreciated by others, or even by themselves. I remember a disturbing moment when Preston was in an ICU and Perry commented, "I wish this was me and not Preston." Why would he say such a thing? Perry suffered a private and internal grief that we will never know about or fully understand. Perhaps no one said it better than Antoine de Sainte Exupéry in his novella *The Little Prince*: "It's such a secret place, the land of tears." So true.

So how does one grieve for someone who is not dead? I hope that some-day I will learn more fully the answer to this complex question.

Ted and I are resigned—and let me quickly emphasize—we are recon-ciled—to the fact that we will be caring for Preston for the rest of our living days. We are fine with that. I do not want to go to my grave without knowing that I had absolutely done every possible thing to help my oldest son to have the best life possible given his circumstances. If our plans, Ted's and mine, had been to do a lot of traveling together to the beautiful places around the world after we retired, those plans have really only been transformed by the added goal of enriching Preston's life experience by sharing that travel with him. In fact, with his periodic reliance on his wheelchair or other supports, we have found that cruises afford an excellent way of getting him from place to place very easily, while making him comfortable while traveling between destinations while on board. We even use this experience as a therapy by walking Preston around the ship where he also has to work on his balance as the ship sways back and forth.

However, it would be negligent of me not to say that this devastating injury caused by the violent game of football comes without daily struggles for Preston as well as for me and Ted. While loving Preston is very easy and extremely rewarding, he does require 24/7 care. His personal care can be demanding and sometimes very wearing on Ted and I, we are no spring chickens. He can never be left alone for fear of choking or falling. He has even fallen on me trying to help him and we both were subsequently injured. Earlier this year he suffered his worst fall to date which fractured the neck of his femur, broke and dislocated his middle finger and slashed his face requiring stitches. Ted and I were just a few feet away from him when he fell and could not prevent the fall from happening in time. He cannot perform any chores, make himself something to eat, shower, or even dress himself. Since his cognitive and verbal processing is very slow Ted and I have had to learn patience and understanding to actively prevent ourselves from not letting him at least try and do these things for himself. Washing sheets and bed pads is almost an everyday occurrence. In addition, outside of doctor appointments and treatments mentioned earlier, for over ten years we have taken Preston to the gym every Monday through Friday for an hour with a trainer for strength training to keep his muscles functioning to prevent atrophy.

As I mentioned earlier, we also adamantly refuse to give up our ongoing search for treatments, or physical/cognitive therapies, or new drug formulations that might benefit our son. I am constantly on the computer searching for the latest scientific medical advances in the realm of brain, nerve, and spinal cord damage in our unrelenting hope that one day the research will yield procedures or remedies that might significantly improve Preston's situation.

I think it is fair to say that the three of us, and Perry too I hope, fully intend to wring as much enjoyment out of life as possible in the days and years going forward.

* * * *

"Advocacy" to change "what is" to "what should be."

In writing this book, it is not my intention to completely condemn the game of football or to call for its banishment. (Although, who could blame me if I might actually be delighted if football was ever denounced and determined to be too risky a sport, such that it would fade away into extinction?) Rather, my purpose, most fundamentally, is to increase awareness by educating parents, coaches, and trainers—and when they are old enough to understand, the players themselves—about the risks and dangers for serious brain injuries that they face every moment when they play the game of football, as well as other contact sports too. In particular, I want to focus parental attention on their young children and teenager players who face the greatest risk simply because their brains are not fully formed and are therefore far more susceptible to serious injury from even moderate hits on the field.

Throughout the years after Preston's injury, I have advocated for rules and regulations to be changed and enforced in all sports in response to the dangers posed by concussions and their after-effects, because if you don't ask for change, it will be assumed that you don't want or need it. "Silence will not protect you"; an aphorism that says it best. In response to Preston's injury, the NCAA implemented new guidelines to tackle the concussion controversy. However, these are just guidelines, suggestions if you will, and with no repercussions for failure to comply.

In March of 2008, I testified in Trenton New Jersey before the New Jersey State Board of Education, arguing in favor of legislation to adopt a standardized policy for treating and monitoring concussions. I was pleased that in 2010, then Governor Chris Christie signed assembly bill A-2743; legislation requiring the Department of Education to develop an athletic head injury safety training program(s) for all public and non-public schools. This legislation requires that all high school and collegiate football programs must institute proactive, on-field concussion management protocols specifically designed to identify potentially serious head or brain injuries, and to get any players suspected to have sustained them off the field and out of the game without being permitted to return.

Coaches and trainers also should be required to undergo formal training that will enable them quickly and effectively to spot the symptoms of concussion as well as knowing how to properly administer sideline diagnostic tests like the Standardized Assessment of Concussion (SAC) test battery. Furthermore, players who do sustain on-field head injuries, whether in games or during practice, must be examined by a medical doctor, preferably immediately but in all cases as soon as possible after the event, and they should be expressly prohibited from returning to any manner of play (including practice) until they have been cleared by a qualified medical practitioner, preferably a neurologist.

In May of 2010 I also appeared before the House Judiciary Committee in New York City along with two of the NFL's Medical Committee Co-Chairmen, as well as several retired NFL players and doctors. My intent at this meeting was to present Preston's personal story, the face of consequence resulting from the lack of any reasonable concussion protocol, which ultimately led to his devastating Second Impact Syndrome (SIS). In addition, to continue my efforts regarding the dangers of concussions and SIS, I have spoken at events sponsored by such organizations or institutions as the New Jersey Brain Association, NJ Children's Hospital, the Kiwanis Club, ARC, and Pop Warner, as well as contributing to numerous newspaper articles to bring attention to this serious problem within the athletic community, and particularly for the sake of our children.

It is important to point out that none of this may be regarded as placing some sort of onerous burden on the people and institutions (such as the NCAA and the NFL) who are responsible for overseeing and directing incredibly successful organized football programs across America—widely celebrated, media-saturating programs that generate billions of dollars in revenue every year from everything ranging from game attendance to product advertising and endorsements. When you come right down to it, all I am asking is that concussion injuries be given just as much attention and scrutiny and medical care as broken bones and torn muscles or ligaments.

Although, when you really think about it, there really is no doubt that concussion injuries should be given just a little bit more attention. Because the truth is, broken bones and torn muscles, for the most part, heal 100 percent completely. But serious concussions that lead to traumatic brain injury, or that open the possibility of even more catastrophic and life-long debilitating injuries like second impact syndrome (SIS) and chronic traumatic encephalopathy (CTE)—as we have seen in this book—these are the forever injuries.

Let's face it and be honest here, playing football is a gamble. It's about taking a risk, facing the odds while competing for a coveted result. Preston as well as many other athletes before him—and unfortunately there will be others to come after him—have taken this risk and have lost. My hope and purpose with this book is that you will think about Preston if you or someone you know should suffer a concussion, and that you will take the immediate steps necessary to seriously address this brain injury to allow sufficient time—more than sufficient time—for complete healing before returning to sports. I also highly recommend that you please visit the website of the CDC Center for Disease Control and Prevention (cdc.gov) and click on the "HEADS UP to Youth Sports" page for specific concussion information that is vital for coaches, parents, sports officials and especially young athletes. Concussions are a real fact. Second Impact Syndrome is a real fact. Death from football is a real fact. Athletes developing CTE is a real fact. Remember, you only get one brain; it is critically important that you take care of it. Are you willing to gamble with your life or your loved one's life?

My firm belief is that highlighting awareness of the risks and consequences of concussion injuries from playing football is absolutely crucial as the best means for enlightening everyone who is in any way connected with or involved in the game, ultimately so that no other young child, teenager or adult athlete will ever be forced to sit out, like my boy Preston, for the rest of their lives.

I demolish the bridges
behind me

then....

there is no choice but to
move forward

Fridtjof Nansen